# Terraform for Developers

## Second Edition

***Essentials of Infrastructure Automation and Provisioning***

AF669223

*Kimiko Lee*

Published by: GitforGits

Publisher: Sonal Dhandre

www.gitforgits.com

support@gitforgits.com

Printed in India

First Printing: October 2024

ISBN: 978-81-19177-86-8

Cover Design by: Kitten Publishing

# Prologue

Terraform stands as the leader in Infrastructure as Code, empowering developers and operators to automate, adjust, and refine their infrastructure at a fast pace. I, Kimiko Lee, share this second edition to support those who want to transform static or repetitive setups into nimble environments that respond to today's demands. When I look back on everything Terraform has enabled since its early releases, I see how far we've come: from simple "here's a VM" usage to advanced patterns that unify container orchestration, ephemeral secrets, and specialized add-ons. This evolution is precisely why I felt compelled to revise my original edition and bring it to you with an updated edition that captures the latest practices.

In this book, you'll follow a steady progression from foundational principles—variables, plans, and modular thinking—into deeper territory like dynamic secrets management, ephemeral infrastructure, and multi-environment pipelines. My aim is not to overwhelm you but to demonstrate that Terraform's strength lies in tackling real situations. I will get you skilled to create modules that the entire team can share, so we avoid rewriting the same definitions whenever we deploy new services. I will take you to how ephemeral credentials from Vault reduce the headache of storing or rotating long-lived secrets. We will explore networking constructs in the cloud to show that you can unify subnets, routes, and load balancers under Terraform's single framework. In the later chapters, you'll explore to spin up entire Kubernetes clusters and even manage container images and metadata without scattering references across different scripts or files.

Throughout our book, I made sure to use practical code snippets, scenario-based examples, and step-by-step instructions. I've made sure to show pitfalls as well, including the confusion that arises with runtime errors or concurrency collisions. It's one thing to see how easy it is to run terraform apply when everything lines up. It's another to diagnose partial success or fix a state lock that's blocking your pipeline. I don't shy away from those topics because understanding how to debug is essential to feeling confident when real deadlines loom.

When I first drafted all these topics for this second edition, my objective was to deliver the skills I learned the hard way, so you can skip frustration and jump directly to more interesting solutions. This second edition builds on that promise, refined by countless hours of speaking with teams who overcame the same challenges. I believe in a living approach to infrastructure, where code evolves, deployments adapt, and missteps become the impetus for improvement.

***My hope is that, by reading, experimenting, and applying these chapters, you'll feel that Terraform transforms the mundane aspects of deployment into a creative, high-impact practice.***

***--Kimiko Lee***

# Content

# Preface

This is the second edition of the Terraform for Developers book, presenting a thoroughly practical approach to using IaC for robust deployment and maintenance. This latest release is the most updated edition on Terraform, with the latest capabilities, patterns, and hands-on applications. Each chapter breaks down complex ideas into easy-to-follow steps, showing how to deal with the real challenges that come up in modern cloud deployments.

You'll start by learning the basics, like providers, variables, and states. It also highlights some really cool modules, showing how to create, reuse, and share them across projects. Later on, it covers secrets management, showing how to store and handle sensitive data safely. It also covers advanced networking and multi-cloud usage, hurdles in bridging subnets, load balancers, and container orchestration frameworks. It also covers troubleshooting across the syntax, logic, and runtime issues that might occur. And it shows how to incorporate testing, from unit checks on modules to integration scenarios for multi-service environments.

The final chapters cover advanced topics such as customizing workflows with CI/CD pipelines and using test environments. This book won't turn you into a Terraform master overnight, but it will show you all the practical features, patterns, and tricks to improve your infrastructure management.

In this book you will learn how to:

- Discover how Terraform streamlines resource provisioning.
- Write maintainable modules with confidence.
- Integrate advanced network constructs, subnets, and routing logic across multi-cloud topologies.
- Employ ephemeral credentials with Vault dynamic secrets.
- Automate robust tests, from unit checks to full environment validations.
- Practical debugging steps for syntax, semantic, and runtime errors.
- Adopt CI/CD pipelines to unify code reviews and automated deployments.
- Combine container orchestration solutions with Terraform's consistent state tracking to scale clusters.
- Structure microservices, security, and multi-environment usage.
- Track resource utilization, concurrency, and code maintainability across your stack.

# GitforGits

## Prerequisites

This book brings all the capabilities Terraform has to offer, in much practical and easy understanding manner. It is a must read by all developers, programmers and cloud administrators who some or the other means get in connection to work with Terraform. All you need is som knowledge about the infrastructure and some coding experience to sail through this book.

## Codes Usage

Are you in need of some helpful code examples to assist you in your programming and documentation? Look no further! Our book offers a wealth of supplemental material, including code examples and exercises.

Not only is this book here to aid you in getting your job done, but you have our permission to use the example code in your programs and documentation. However, please note that if you are reproducing a significant portion of the code, we do require you to contact us for permission.

But don't worry, using several chunks of code from this book in your program or answering a question by citing our book and quoting example code does not require permission. But if you do choose to give credit, an attribution typically includes the title, author, publisher, and ISBN. For example, "Terraform for Developers, Second Edition by Kimiko Lee".

If you are unsure whether your intended use of the code examples falls under fair use or the permissions outlined above, please do not hesitate to reach out to us at support@gitforgits.com.

We are happy to assist and clarify any concerns.

# Acknowledgement

I owe a tremendous debt of gratitude to GitforGits, for their unflagging enthusiasm and wise counsel throughout the entire process of writing this book. Their knowledge and careful editing helped make sure the piece was useful for people of all reading levels and comprehension skills. In addition, I'd like to thank everyone involved in the publishing process for their efforts in making this book a reality. Their efforts, from copyediting to advertising, made the project what it is today.

Finally, I'd like to express my gratitude to everyone who has shown me unconditional love and encouragement throughout my life. Their support was crucial to the completion of this book. I appreciate your help with this endeavour and your continued interest in my career.

# Chapter 1: Introduction to Terraform and IaC

# Introduction to Terraform and IaC

Infrastructure as Code, popularly known as IaC, represents a significant shift in infrastructure management by leveraging concepts traditionally associated with software development. Before the adoption of IaC, infrastructure management was largely manual, where system administrators would configure servers, networks, storage, and other resources by hand. This traditional approach often led to inconsistencies, errors, and prolonged deployment cycles. One of the most common issues in manual setups was the "it works on my machine" scenario, which caused conflicts and instability across development, testing, and production environments. It emerged to address these challenges, applying software engineering practices—such as version control, code review, automated testing, and continuous integration—to the realm of IT infrastructure. In IaC, the entire infrastructure is defined, provisioned, managed, and deployed using code. This enables automation, repeatability, and consistency in infrastructure management. Additionally, because infrastructure is codified, it becomes easier to detect and rectify discrepancies between environments, resulting in more stable and predictable systems.

## IaC Evolution

Initially, IaC practices involved basic server configuration tools such as Chef, Puppet, and Ansible. These tools marked the first generation of IaC solutions, primarily focusing on automating repetitive tasks associated with configuring individual servers or server clusters. This methodology, known as **`mutable infrastructure`**, involved continually updating existing servers, often leading to issues such as configuration drift—where servers gradually deviated from their desired state.

The limitations associated with mutable infrastructure drove the evolution towards **`immutable infrastructure`**, a model adopted by modern IaC tools like Terraform, AWS CloudFormation, and Google Cloud Deployment Manager. Immutable infrastructure fundamentally changes the management approach: infrastructure components are never modified after their initial deployment. Instead, any required updates trigger the destruction of the existing resources and provisioning of entirely new ones. This practice significantly reduces the possibility of drift, thus increasing the reliability and consistency of infrastructure deployments.

## Introduction to Terraform

Terraform is an open-source tool developed by HashiCorp, has become a leading solution in managing infrastructure via code, specifically embracing immutable infrastructure practices. Terraform enables developers and system administrators to describe infrastructure resources using a clear and concise declarative language known as HashiCorp Configuration Language (HCL). This language is intuitive and easily readable by humans, making it accessible even to those without extensive infrastructure backgrounds.

The approach of Terraform is fundamentally declarative, meaning you specify the desired end state of your infrastructure rather than describing procedural steps to achieve it. Terraform then handles provisioning, updating, and maintaining resources based on this desired state definition. Its platform-agnostic capability allows users to manage resources across diverse environments, including major cloud providers like AWS, Azure, and Google Cloud, as well as on-premises platforms like VMware and OpenStack. Additionally, Terraform's extensive community-developed provider ecosystem ensures continuous support for new platforms and technologies.

Another distinctive feature of Terraform is its modularity. Terraform encourages code reuse through modules, enabling teams to encapsulate complex configurations into reusable units. This modular approach simplifies infrastructure management, fosters collaboration, reduces code redundancy, and eases the management of intricate systems such as microservices architectures.

## Advantages and Merits of IaC

The implementation of IaC brings numerous benefits, dramatically improving the ways organizations manage their IT infrastructure. Below are several critical advantages and merits IaC provides to development and operations teams:

- Speed and Operational Efficiency

With IaC, tasks that traditionally took significant time and effort—such as provisioning servers, configuring network components, and deploying applications—can now be completed within minutes. Automation via IaC enables rapid and parallel deployment of resources, freeing developers to focus more intensely on writing application logic rather than performing manual infrastructure setups.

- Consistency and Reliability

Manual processes are prone to human error, leading to inconsistent infrastructure states. By defining infrastructure in code, IaC eliminates variations between environments. The same configuration code is consistently applied to development, testing, staging, and production, dramatically reducing environment-related issues and providing more predictable deployments.

- Enhanced Scalability and Flexibility

IaC allows infrastructure scaling through simple adjustments within code configurations. Scaling up or down, deploying replicas of existing environments for testing or disaster recovery purposes, or accommodating changes in resource demands becomes straightforward. Terraform and similar tools offer flexibility in supporting diverse technology stacks, enabling teams to swiftly adapt to changing requirements or technology shifts.

- Improved Collaboration and Transparency

Codified infrastructure serves as a single source of truth, improving transparency and collaboration among teams. Operations and development teams collaborate seamlessly, reviewing and enhancing infrastructure code in a unified manner. This cross-functional approach helps align team objectives, significantly improving workflow efficiency and understanding.

- Version Control and Enhanced Auditability

One of IaC's strongest merits is integrating version control systems (such as Git) to manage infrastructure code. Every modification to the infrastructure configuration can be tracked, reviewed, and reverted if necessary. This integration supports compliance requirements, simplifies troubleshooting, and provides a detailed audit trail, especially critical in regulated environments or sensitive industries.

- Cost Optimization and Resource Efficiency

IaC introduces significant cost efficiencies. Automating infrastructure management reduces labor costs, and dynamic scaling ensures optimal resource utilization. Infrastructure resources can be provisioned or de-provisioned on-demand, preventing wastage associated with over-provisioning or idle resources. Additionally, temporary environments (such as testing environments) can be spun up and torn down automatically, substantially reducing unnecessary expenditure.

- Risk Mitigation and Improved Disaster Recovery

IaC minimizes risks associated with manual intervention. Because infrastructure is represented as code, organizations can rapidly recover infrastructure states after failures or disasters. By rerunning validated IaC scripts, complete infrastructures can be recreated quickly and accurately, simplifying disaster recovery processes and reducing system downtime.

- Robust Testing and Validation Capabilities

IaC enables comprehensive infrastructure testing practices. By codifying infrastructure definitions, organizations can validate environments before deploying them to production. Automated infrastructure tests, including compliance, security, and performance validations, allow teams to proactively identify and remediate potential issues, ensuring a smooth and error-free deployment experience.

- Immutable Infrastructure Approach

IaC strongly supports immutable infrastructure practices, wherein infrastructure resources are never directly modified after deployment. Instead, resources are replaced entirely with new deployments when changes are required. This strategy effectively eliminates configuration drift and increases infrastructure stability and predictability.

- Self-Documenting Infrastructure

Infrastructure code inherently serves as documentation, clearly outlining the configuration, resources, dependencies, and interactions. This embedded documentation significantly reduces the overhead traditionally associated with creating separate infrastructure documentation, simplifying team onboarding and maintaining clarity about the current infrastructure state.

- Environment Parity across Development Stages

IaC simplifies the creation of identical environments across different stages of software delivery (development, testing, staging, and production). Achieving consistent environments minimizes discrepancies that often lead to deployment issues, increasing the stability and predictability of software releases.

So, by adopting IaC—especially with Terraform—organizations can effectively handle not just any infrastructure, but increasingly complex and ever-changing ones. Terraform really delivers on the promises of IaC thanks to its declarative approach, extensibility, the fact that it's agnostic to the cloud, its robust community, and its extensive integration capabilities. All these features make Terraform a great pick for development and operations teams looking for reliable, scalable, efficient, and future-proof infrastructure management solutions.

# Elements of IaC

IaC capabilities are built on foundational elements that each address different aspects of infrastructure management. These elements allow teams to scale their automation practices as environments grow in size and complexity. Following are the key elements that completes the power of IaC:

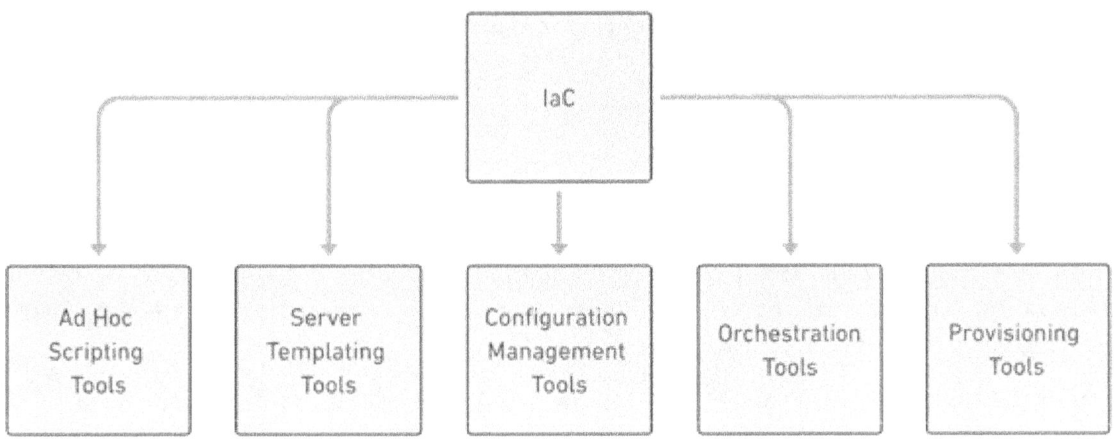


**Fig.1.1 Key Components of IaC**

- Ad Hoc Scripting

Ad hoc scripting marks the starting point for many teams venturing into IaC. It involves writing scripts—often in shell, PowerShell, or Python—to automate repetitive tasks such as installing packages or creating user accounts. Although these scripts simplify routine operations, they typically lack platform independence and idempotency, so running them multiple times may produce inconsistent outcomes. Additionally, ad hoc scripts often require manual execution, reducing their effectiveness for large-scale or continuous automation needs. Nonetheless, they provide a straightforward entry into automation, especially for organizations beginning to reduce manual intervention.

- Server Templating

Server templating builds on scripting by offering predefined images or container-based templates that define a server's state. Tools like Packer, Docker, or Vagrant capture operating systems, installed software, and configurations within these templates, ensuring consistent deployments across diverse environments. By packaging server configurations into version-controlled files, teams avoid inconsistencies tied to manual setup, reducing integration headaches and misconfiguration errors. However, server templating alone does not address certain higher-level tasks, such as orchestrating dependencies between services or continuously enforcing a desired configuration. For more comprehensive needs, advanced IaC solutions are often preferable.

- Configuration Management

Configuration management solutions (Puppet, Chef, Ansible, SaltStack) broaden IaC by defining and maintaining desired infrastructure states over time. Instead of focusing solely on isolated servers or images, these tools manage entire infrastructures through a declarative approach, where users specify the target configuration for operating systems, installed applications, and services. By continuously comparing the current environment to the specified configuration, they rapidly reconcile any differences. This prevents drift, ensures consistent deployment standards, and simplifies maintenance of large-scale systems. Additionally, most tools in this category handle interdependencies among resources, sequencing updates to avoid conflicts.

- Orchestration

Orchestration solutions—Kubernetes, Docker Swarm, Apache Mesos—serve a specialized role in managing containerized workloads. They automatically schedule container instances, balance resources, maintain desired container counts, and handle communication across distributed services. While these tools often operate atop infrastructure provisioned by IaC solutions, they optimize the runtime behavior of microservices, scaling containerized applications on demand. Orchestration complements provisioning by focusing on how services run and interact, ensuring high availability, resilience, and efficient resource utilization.

- Provisioning

Provisioning tools supply the most comprehensive IaC capabilities, enabling the definition and lifecycle management of networks, virtual machines, load balancers, databases, and other infrastructure components. Terraform, AWS CloudFormation, and Google Cloud Deployment Manager fall under this category. Terraform stands out for its cloud-agnostic nature, unifying the management of resources across different platforms with a single workflow. Such tools maintain a detailed representation (or state) of deployed infrastructure, allowing consistent tracking of changes, reducing human error, and simplifying repetitive or large-scale deployments.

The teams primarily and majorly incorporate multiple IaC elements in their work environment. They may begin with simple scripts, adopt server templating, or add configuration management to sustain reliable states. Gradually, they evolve into end-to-end provisioning and orchestration solutions that fully automate their environments and enable modern delivery practices.

# Core Principles of Terraform

Terraform rests on core principles that streamline provisioning, updates, and maintenance. Its popularity arises from these key ideas, which simplify large-scale environments, reduce risk, and unify multi-cloud or hybrid strategies.

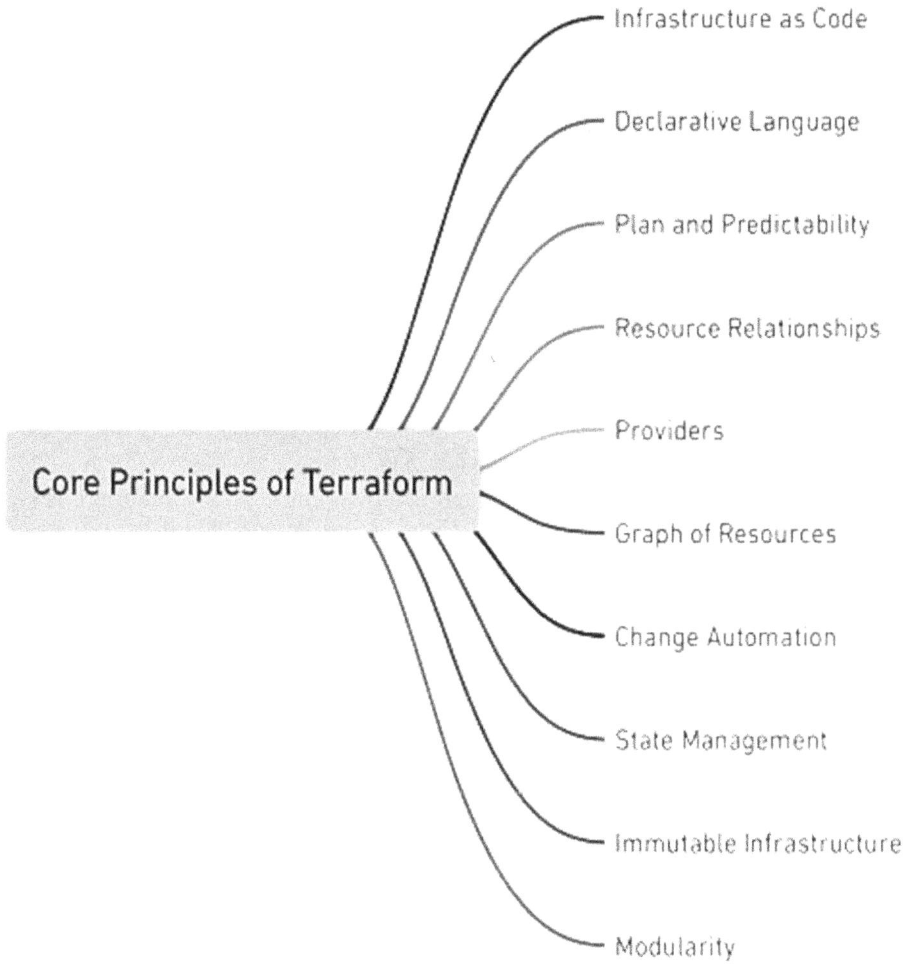


**Fig 1.2 Core Principles of Terraform**

## *Code-Centric Model*

Terraform codifies infrastructure as high-level, human-readable configuration files using HCL. This brings version control, peer review, and testing—hallmarks of software engineering—into infrastructure management. Rather than manually setting up each resource, users define them in code, promoting consistency, reuse, and collaborative workflows.

### *Declarative Language*

Terraform follows a declarative paradigm rather than prescribing procedural steps. The users specify desired state of each resource—such as computing instances, networking rules, or storage systems—and Terraform automatically determines how to achieve that state. This abstraction allows teams to focus on outcomes, leaving the intricacies of infrastructure orchestration to Terraform's engine.

### *Plan and Predictability*

The **`terraform plan`** command exemplifies Terraform's emphasis on clarity and safety. It generates a detailed report of any additions, modifications, or deletions required to reconcile the actual infrastructure with the code. Teams can review this plan, confirm changes, or abort if something seems incorrect. This feedback loop fosters predictable, controlled deployments, reducing unanticipated disruptions.

### *Resource Relationships and Dependencies*

Terraform comprehends dependencies through explicit references between resources, ensuring the correct sequence of creation, updates, or destruction. Dependencies might include linking virtual machines to a network, associating a database with a storage volume, or configuring security rules for an instance. Terraform's ability to handle these relationships frees teams from painstakingly tracking complex resource orders.

### *Providers and Extensible Architecture*

Providers link Terraform to various platforms or services, including AWS, Azure, Google Cloud, VMware, and Kubernetes. This extensible architecture allows rapid adoption of new providers or services without altering Terraform's core. Each provider encapsulates a set of resources and data sources, letting organizations compose complex infrastructures by mixing providers across multiple clouds or on-premises environments.

### *Graph of Resources*

Under the hood, Terraform constructs a dependency graph to map relationships between all defined resources. It can provision or update non-dependent resources in parallel, significantly accelerating large deployments. This graph also enforces the correct order for interdependent resources, preventing errors or partial updates that might compromise the stability of live systems.

### *Change Automation and Infrastructure Updates*

Automating infrastructure changes is a central Terraform principle. The tool compares the current state to the desired state, then generates and executes a plan to fix any discrepancies. This automation eliminates repetitive, error-prone manual tasks, enabling rapid iterative changes aligned with DevOps workflows. As infrastructure evolves, Terraform consistently applies updates, ensuring that production remains in sync with code.

### *Robust State Management*

Terraform maintains an authoritative state file capturing resource metadata and dependencies, keeping track of how it maps to real-world components. By referencing this file, Terraform accurately determines the operations necessary to achieve the declared environment. Teams typically store state files in remote backends for secure access, team collaboration, and audit trails.

### *Immutable Infrastructure Approach*

Terraform promotes immutable infrastructure principles, where replacing resources rather than patching them minimizes drift and lowers maintenance overhead. This eliminates hidden changes that accumulate over time, making environments simpler to replicate, validate, and troubleshoot. Immutable strategies also allow rapid rollbacks or environment rebuilds if unexpected errors arise.

### *Modularity and Reusability*

Terraform integrates modules that group multiple resources into reusable blocks. Organizations maintain libraries of modules—covering everything from standard virtual machines to complex networking designs—enabling consistent best practices across teams and reducing duplication. Modules simplify large projects, cut down on repeated code, and facilitate knowledge sharing within or between teams.

# Architecture of Terraform

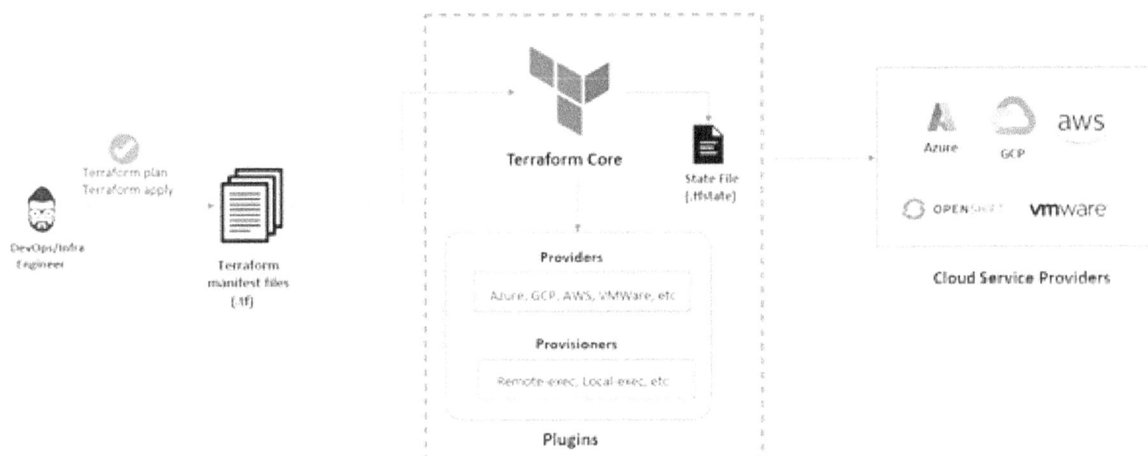


**Fig 1.3 Terraform Architecture**

*Source: https://spacelift.io/blog/terraform-architecture*

## Core Engine and Plugin Framework

The architecture of Terraform centers on a core engine that processes configuration files and a plugin framework that extends its capabilities to different platforms and services. The core engine is responsible for interpreting HCL, building a dependency graph of resources, and determining how to reconcile the desired infrastructure state with the actual environment. This mechanism involves reading each resource definition, assessing dependencies, and orchestrating the creation, modification, or destruction of resources. While the core focuses on these general functions, providers implement the specific logic for interacting with external APIs such as AWS, Azure, Google Cloud, or on-premises solutions like VMware. Each provider has an interface that describes how resources are created, updated, read, or deleted. The modular nature of the plugin framework keeps the Terraform executable lightweight and adaptable. As new platforms or technologies emerge, you only need updated providers to manage those resources, rather than altering Terraform's core. This separation of concerns allows Terraform to remain flexible for a wide range of environments.

## Resource Graph and State Management

The resource graph is a foundational component of Terraform's architecture, mapping out how different infrastructure elements relate to one another and establishing the correct execution order. When the core engine reads configuration files, it identifies dependencies, such as a virtual machine's reliance on a network or a database's requirement for storage, forming a directional graph. Terraform then executes resource operations in a sequence that respects these dependencies, parallelizing non-dependent tasks for efficiency. This approach is particularly helpful in complex environments with numerous microservices or large sets of interlinked resources. Alongside the resource graph, Terraform maintains a state file that tracks metadata for all resources under management, mapping configuration definitions to live infrastructure objects. This state file is paramount for ensuring Terraform knows whether changes have occurred, preventing duplication or drift in real-world deployments. Teams often store state remotely in secure, shared backends, enabling collaborative workflows and protecting against inconsistencies introduced by multiple individuals updating infrastructure at the same time.

## Providers and Provisioners

Providers are the linchpins connecting Terraform's core with external services or platforms. Each provider supports a range of resource types relevant to its domain, from cloud instances and serverless functions to DNS records and managed databases. This design lets you manage diverse infrastructures—cloud-based or otherwise—within a single, unified workflow. Provisioners, meanwhile, offer a way to run local or remote actions on a resource during creation or destruction. Some users leverage provisioners for tasks like bootstrapping software or generating configuration files that cannot easily be managed by standard resource definitions. However, heavy use of provisioners can signal that a dedicated provider or configuration management tool might be more suitable. Providers and provisioners both extend Terraform's functionality beyond simple resource declarations, accommodating a wide range of scenarios. Their inherent flexibility also grants administrators the freedom to integrate Terraform with evolving or niche technologies, ensuring infrastructure remains consistent even when spread across heterogeneous platforms.

## Terraform CLI

The Terraform CLI is the command-line interface through which you can create, modify, and destroy infrastructure. Commands like **`terraform init`**, **`terraform plan`**, and **`terraform apply`** make it possible to manage resources in a predictable and stepwise fashion. During initialization, Terraform configures providers, downloads necessary plugins, and prepares the backend for storing state. When the plan command is executed, the CLI evaluates differences between the desired state defined in code and the current real-world environment, showing an itemized list of operations—like adding or removing resources—required to achieve alignment. You can carefully review these actions to avoid unintended modifications before running **`terraform apply`**, which commits the changes and updates the state file accordingly. The CLI also includes features for output variables, module management, and workspace handling, all of which improve your ability to oversee environments at scale. By focusing on clarity and transparency, the CLI ensures teams maintain a tight feedback loop regarding infrastructure status and proposed adjustments.

## Workspaces and Modules

Workspaces and modules are two architectural concepts that help Terraform scale within large organizations or projects. Workspaces allow teams to manage multiple state files for a single configuration, providing a practical method to handle parallel environments (development, staging, production) without duplicating code. Each workspace maintains its own state, ensuring that changes in one environment do not inadvertently affect others. Meanwhile, modules encapsulate sets of resources into reusable packages. This approach promotes standardization and consistency across repeated configurations, as teams can share modules for common tasks like creating virtual networks, setting up security groups, or provisioning managed databases. Modules can be hosted in private or public registries, where teams can version, audit, and improve them over time. By integrating workspaces and modules, Terraform's architecture makes it possible to maintain a single source of truth for complex infrastructures while still allowing environment-specific customizations, ultimately simplifying large-scale deployments and maintenance.

## Remote Backends and Collaboration

Remote backends and collaborative features further enhance Terraform's architectural flexibility by separating state storage from local environments. You can configure a backend such as AWS S3, Azure Blob Storage, HashiCorp Consul, or Terraform Cloud to store the state file centrally. This setup lets multiple team members run commands against the same infrastructure definitions without corrupting state or overwriting changes. Locking mechanisms prevent concurrent modifications, while versioning and logging capabilities enhance auditability. Teams can also integrate Terraform with continuous integration pipelines, automatically applying changes after code is merged into a main branch, provided the plan output passes review. This combination of remote state, locking, and CI-based workflows enables truly collaborative infrastructure management. The architecture remains open-ended, allowing different organizations to adopt a workflow that fits their needs, whether fully automated, semi-manual, or something in between. By aligning with DevOps principles, Terraform's remote backend support encourages consistent, repeatable deployments and fosters transparency across distributed teams.

# Terraform Key Features

## Multi-Platform and Cloud-Agnostic Approach

Terraform's strongest feature is its unified interface for managing resources across diverse platforms. Organizations often rely on multiple clouds to gain flexibility, cost advantages, or regional coverage, yet managing these infrastructures can be complicated if each provider uses distinct tooling. Terraform streamlines this by offering a common configuration language and command set, bridging public clouds, private virtualization platforms, container orchestration services, and Software as a Service integration. This flexibility allows DevOps teams to define complex topologies spanning different providers in a single configuration, including hybrid setups that merge on-premises infrastructure with cloud resources. Having a single workflow reduces the learning curve for you, minimizes the overhead of switching between platforms, and provides a consistent way of version-controlling and reviewing infrastructure changes.

## Declarative Syntax and Predictable Workflows

Declarative syntax is foundational to Terraform's design, allowing you to specify what the infrastructure should look like rather than describing step-by-step procedures. This distinction removes the need for detailed instructions about how to create and interconnect resources. Instead, Terraform compares the current state with the desired state, deciding how to achieve alignment without manual oversight. Along with this declarative approach, Terraform emphasizes predictable workflows through commands like **`terraform plan`** and **`terraform apply`**. The plan command is integral to safe and cautious operations because it displays a preview of all proposed changes—additions, modifications, deletions—before anything is finalized. You can confirm correctness, detect potential mistakes, and decide whether adjustments should proceed. If approvals are granted, the apply command runs, implementing changes and updating state. This workflow brings thorough visibility into actions and fosters a culture of review, version control, and peer collaboration to maintain stable and well-documented environments over time.

## Immutability and Reproducible Environments

Terraform aligns with immutable infrastructure principles by favoring replacement of resources over in-place alterations. This design choice prevents hidden configuration mismatches or leftover artifacts that accumulate when systems are continually patched rather than replaced. By adopting immutability, teams can test updates in parallel environments before switching traffic over to the new infrastructure. Should issues emerge, rolling back is as simple as switching to a previous version. This eliminates problems often associated with partial upgrades or unintentional drift. Immutability also promotes consistency in ephemeral environments used for development or testing, making it straightforward to spin up exact replicas of production for experimentation or quality assurance. Such reproducible infrastructure drastically reduces the "it works on my machine" issue, because the code that defines production can be used to create a reliable clone for debugging or performance testing.

## State Tracking and Intelligent Change Management

State tracking is at the heart of Terraform's functionality, giving it awareness of resource attributes and relationships in a way that streamlines change management. Once the desired configuration is declared, Terraform looks at its state file to determine what is already running in the environment and what is missing or requires updates. This knowledge of current conditions enables Terraform to create minimal, targeted plans to fix discrepancies, significantly reducing the risk of unintended side effects. The state file maintains resource identifiers, metadata, and outputs that can be shared among modules or references in other parts of the configuration. By updating this state whenever changes are applied, Terraform maintains a living record of infrastructure evolution. The ability to store state in remote backends, along with locking features, lets distributed teams coordinate securely.

## Data Sources and Extended Integrations

Terraform extends beyond raw resource creation by providing data sources and integrations that further enrich the scope of automation. Data sources allow you to fetch information from existing infrastructure or external systems, making it possible to dynamically populate configuration variables rather than hard-coding them. This capability simplifies multi-step deployments that rely on details such as IP addresses, networking metadata, or reference IDs produced by other processes. Terraform also offers ways to integrate with tools like configuration management solutions and third-party systems for advanced scenarios. If a specialized service is not directly accessible through existing providers, custom or community-driven providers can be developed to bridge the gap. This ecosystem approach allows Terraform to accommodate evolving technologies without a complete overhaul of internal structures.

## Collaboration, Modularity, and Continuous Delivery

Terraform's feature set is optimized for team-driven workflows that scale well alongside organizational growth. The emphasis on declarative code and version control practices ensures that multiple contributors can collaborate without causing infrastructural inconsistencies. Remote state backends, coupled with locking mechanisms, prevent collisions by ensuring that only one process can modify the state at a time. Modularity takes collaboration a step further, allowing groups of related resources to be packaged as modules. These modules can be versioned, shared, or downloaded from public or private registries, promoting consistency across diverse projects. When combined with continuous integration pipelines, Terraform configurations can be validated and tested just like application code. Teams often incorporate automated checks that run **`terraform plan`** on each pull request, surfacing any changes before they reach production.

## Provider Ecosystem and Ecosystem Tools

The Terraform community actively maintains a broad provider ecosystem, reflecting the diversity of modern IT environments. Teams managing conventional virtualization platforms, container orchestrators like Kubernetes, or specialized SaaS offerings can locate corresponding providers that translate Terraform's standard declarative syntax into API calls specific to each platform. Beyond providers, a wealth of open-source and proprietary tools integrate with Terraform, enhancing functionalities like policy enforcement, drift detection, and secrets management. For instance, some organizations rely on Sentinel or Open Policy Agent to enforce guardrails, ensuring that Terraform plans comply with security or compliance requirements before apply operations take place. Others employ external linting tools or custom scripts to check code quality, naming conventions, or resource tagging. This vibrant ecosystem of plugins and helper utilities amplifies Terraform's capabilities and supports advanced workflows for enterprises.

## Seamless DevOps Adoption

Terraform naturally aligns with the DevOps mentality by providing a predictable, testable, and repeatable model for infrastructure changes. The plan-and-apply workflow forms a loop of feedback and improvement, where every modification can be reviewed in code form and tested before reaching production systems. Teams that value continuous improvement often embed Terraform in a pipeline that automatically provisions ephemeral environments for each new feature branch. Once testing confirms functionality, merging that branch triggers an approved plan-and-apply routine, ensuring that production infrastructure remains in lockstep with the repository's latest code. This approach shortens feedback loops, catches mistakes earlier, and enforces consistent deployments, all of which embody DevOps principles. By tying changes to version control commits, Terraform helps unify developers and you under the same processes. Rather than separate handoffs of environment requests, both teams collaborate on code that defines exactly how infrastructure should evolve to support application features or scale demands.

## Version Control Integration and Auditability

Every resource definition, variable, or module reference is stored as code, meaning that changes can be tracked in systems like Git. Pull requests or merge requests offer a forum for discussions, approvals, or suggested modifications to the infrastructure. This level of traceability and peer review is invaluable in industries subject to regulations or compliance standards, where demonstration of due diligence and change governance is essential. If a deployed modification introduces a problem, teams can revert to a previous commit and reapply Terraform, thereby restoring the environment to a known-good state. The combination of remote state storage and commit history creates a clear record of who changed what and when, streamlining audits, post-incident reviews, and accountability practices. Over time, this forms a knowledge repository that documents an infrastructure's entire lifecycle, clarifying architectural decisions and their impact on operations.

# Summary

So, we started exploring IaC, getting to know its history and how it's a game-changer for modern software development. We talked about how it copies software development practices for managing infrastructure, and it brings perks like code review, version control, and continuous integration and delivery. We took a close look at the different parts of IaC, like ad-hoc scripting, server templating, configuration management, orchestration, and provisioning.

After that, we dug deeper into Terraform, which is considered one of the best IaC tools out there. We explored its key principles, like its declarative language, its ability to plan and predict, its resource relationships, its providers, its state management, and its modularity. We really focused on the idea of declaring the resources we need and letting Terraform handle the rest. Then, we took a look at Terraform's architecture and features. The lifecycle of resources is managed by the core, and plugins, like providers and provisioners, add to Terraform's functionality to handle a bunch of different resources. The whole thing is built around the core and plugins, with the core handling the lifecycle of resources.

Overall, it's a pretty solid tool for dealing with complex infrastructure made up of platform-agnostic nature, its ability to describe changes in advance, the resource graph, and the ability to divide things into modules.

# Chapter 2: Getting Started with Terraform

# Installing Terraform

In the previous chapter, we did familiarize ourselves with the fundamentals of IaC and delved deep into the principles, architecture, and features of Terraform, a leading tool in the IaC landscape. We discovered the power of using declarative language for managing infrastructure, the efficiency of planning and predictability in handling changes, and the importance of state in maintaining consistency and avoiding conflicts. Now, we're ready to roll up our sleeves and get our hands dirty with Terraform.

The first thing we'll do is install Terraform. Terraform is currently on version 1.1.0, but keep in mind that they update it pretty often, so be sure to check the Terraform website for the latest version.

## Downloading and Installing Terraform

We typically begin with an official download from HashiCorp's website to acquire the correct Terraform binary for their operating system. Since we are using linux/ubuntu, we will simply open the terminal and run the following command:

```
wget
https://releases.hashicorp.com/terraform/1.1.0/terraform_1.1.0
_linux_amd64.zip
```

This will retrieve the appropriate archive. A similar approach is used by macOS users, though many prefer Homebrew with a straightforward as given below

```
brew install terraform
```

The Windows users can download the ZIP from their browser, then unzip it in a directory of their choice. The unzipped content generally includes a single file named terraform, which acts as the primary executable. You then move this file into a PATH directory so that the terraform command can be invoked from any folder. Linux systems place it in **/usr/local/bin/**, while Windows users might choose **C:\Windows\System32**. This step ensures that commands like **terraform version** and **terraform init** are recognized globally. It is often best practice to keep a working folder distinct from the Terraform binary location in order to maintain clear boundaries between the infrastructure-as-code projects and system utilities. After placement of the binary, you can run a quick version check to ensure the system recognizes the new command.

Now, there are practical concerns that arise regarding upgrades and version pinning. Although it might suffice to overwrite the old Terraform executable with a newer release, certain teams prefer controlled update processes. These include verifying that infrastructure definitions remain compatible with the new version and ensuring that any novel features or syntax changes do not introduce unexpected behavior. Some workflows keep multiple Terraform versions on the same machine, switching them through environment variables or symlinks. This strategy can be useful for testing older configurations side by side with the latest binaries. Alternatively, package managers such as apt or dnf on Linux, or Scoop and Chocolatey on Windows, can automate updates. Regardless of the approach, once the correct binary is in place, you gain full access to Terraform's capabilities for writing configurations, initializing providers, and interacting with a variety of remote systems.

## Verifying Terraform Installation

Once Terraform is placed in a PATH directory, a rudimentary check can confirm that everything is working. On Linux or macOS, opening a terminal and typing **terraform version** should display details such as Terraform v1.x.x. Windows users can open Command Prompt or PowerShell and do the same. If the command is not recognized, the PATH variable might require adjustment to include the directory holding terraform. In some cases, the user's current session must be reloaded, especially on Windows, for new PATH settings to take effect. Beyond verifying the version, an extra layer of testing can be done by running **terraform --help**, which displays a list of available commands, including **plan**, **apply**, **destroy**, and more. These commands are central to Terraform's operational workflow and confirm that the core functionality is ready.

A helpful next step is to create a simple test configuration within **main.tf** file as below:

```
terraform {
  required_version = ">= 1.0"
}
locals {
  greeting = "Hello Terraform"
}
output "test_message" {
  value = local.greeting
}
```

With this, a local value named **greeting** is defined, and an output block references it. When you run **terraform init**, the working directory will be initialized, though no providers are downloaded because none are declared. Executing **terraform plan** reveals that nothing needs to be created or changed, and **terraform apply** will finalize that empty plan. You can see the test_message output after the apply completes, verifying that Terraform can parse the configuration and produce a result. Although it does not provision real resources, this trivial setup confirms that the binary, environment, and local filesystem are in proper alignment for more advanced configurations.

## Configuring Terraform Path and Environment Variables

Sometimes, setting environment variables is necessary, especially when there are multiple versions of Terraform or when environment-level settings control the behavior of state files and logs. A variable like **TF_LOG** can be set to **DEBUG** to display additional information during plan or apply operations. Linux users might add **export TF_LOG=DEBUG** in their shell configuration file, whereas Windows users may define this variable under system properties. You can often make use of **TF_WORKSPACE** to switch among distinct workspaces for dev, test, or production, each referencing a unique state file.

Another possibility is to define variables for credentials or region settings that integrate seamlessly with certain providers, which can reduce the need to embed sensitive data in code. There are teams who handle secrets or tokens frequently rely on a secure approach that references environment variables in Terraform's configuration.

Following is a quick example:

```
provider "azurerm" {
  features {}
  subscription_id = var.azure_subscription_id
  client_id       = var.azure_client_id
  client_secret   = var.azure_client_secret
  tenant_id       = var.azure_tenant_id
}
```

Here, these **var.azure_*** values could be set by environment variables prefixed with **TF_VAR_** or by a **.tfvars** file kept out of version control. Outside of credentials, environment variables can govern logging verbosity, backend configuration, and other aspects of Terraform's runtime. Each user can adjust these variables to tailor the Terraform experience to personal preferences or organizational constraints. This method fosters consistency, especially when multiple colleagues share an infrastructure codebase. It also means that ephemeral containers, build servers, or remote shells can be dynamically configured for Terraform operations by injecting the necessary environment variables just in time.

## Sample Program: Installation Workflow

Let us practically try out to get the terraform installed in our linux system. Generally, the users might open a terminal and begin by updating local package lists: **sudo apt-get update**.

Although Terraform binaries are not always available in the default repositories, one method is to install **unzip** if it is not already present:

```
sudo apt-get install unzip
```

Then, you can locate the appropriate Terraform release, for instance version 1.2.5, on the HashiCorp releases page. Then copy the direct download URL and run:

```
wget
https://releases.hashicorp.com/terraform/1.2.5/terraform_1.2.5
_linux_amd64.zip
unzip terraform_1.2.5_linux_amd64.zip
sudo mv terraform /usr/local/bin/
```

Upon extracting the zip file, the user moves the Terraform binary into **/usr/local/bin/**, which is already included in the PATH by default. At this point, user can verify the installation with:

```
terraform version
```

If the console displays **Terraform v1.2.5**, the install is successful. An optional step is to store the zip file in a repository of archived tools in case user later decides to roll back versions for compatibility. Some teams also run an automated script that checks for updated releases and performs these tasks.

Once user confirms the correct Terraform version, practical usage begins by creating a new directory for configurations, possibly named **terraform-projects**. Inside that directory, they can test a minimal HCL file and eventually begin more complex definitions that target real cloud infrastructures. With this example, a Linux environment is fully prepared to run Terraform-based provisioning workflows.

# Setting up Azure

## Azure Free Tier and Account Creation

An Azure account is often the entry point for users planning to deploy infrastructure with Terraform on Microsoft's cloud platform. Individuals who do not already have a Microsoft account can register one quickly by visiting the Azure portal sign-up page. A free tier for new signups provides a credit that applies for a limited duration, plus certain services at no charge even after the initial credit has been spent. However, it remains important to keep track of usage to avoid accidental overspending once the free credit expires. During sign-up, Azure requests identity verification, requiring a phone number and valid credit card.

After verifying personal details, you can choose a subscription type. By default, the free tier trial subscription is applied. The Azure Portal then becomes accessible, showing an overview page with pinned shortcuts to common tasks. You might see pre-configured suggestions for spinning up a Windows or Linux VM, creating a database, or exploring advanced features such as serverless functions. The interface includes a left-hand menu with categories for resource groups, app services, virtual networks, storage accounts, and more. Cloud novices might begin with a simple test, like creating a resource group and one virtual machine. This can be done directly in the Portal to explore the platform's interface, or it can be done with Terraform for a fully automated approach.

## Identity Verification and Initial Security

When signing up, Azure will ask for a phone number, which is used for a quick verification code. The credit card details are also validated, usually by placing a small charge that is promptly reversed. These steps confirm that the user is genuine and attempts to prevent unscrupulous activities on the platform. Once the account is active, a good follow-up practice is to enable multi-factor authentication (MFA). That setting can be found in the account security section of the Microsoft account, and it ensures that even if a password is compromised, unauthorized parties cannot easily take over the subscription. In corporate settings, administrators may enforce MFA across all accounts tied to a single Azure tenant, improving security for every team member.

It is also beneficial to acquaint oneself with Azure's RBAC. By default, the user who created the subscription is granted broad privileges, but it might be wise to define additional role assignments if multiple users are collaborating. For instance, an Azure account might have a limited user role that allows usage of existing resources but denies creation or destruction of critical assets. Terraform itself requires specific permissions to create resource groups, networks, or any object in Azure, so a service principal or managed identity with a contributor role is usually created. This identity is then stored in Terraform's provider settings. In practice, it is best to delegate only the minimal privileges required for the code's provisioning tasks.

## Azure CLI and Service Principal Configuration

Many Terraform-based workflows rely on the Azure CLI for authentication and resource management. The CLI, once installed, allows commands like **`az login`**, which prompt the user to authenticate via a browser. After the sign-in process, the CLI can programmatically query or manipulate Azure resources. Installing this tool on Linux or macOS typically involves a script from Microsoft's official repository or a package manager like Homebrew. Windows users can rely on an MSI or the Microsoft Store. Once the CLI is functional, you can often confirm connectivity by listing existing subscriptions with **`az account list`**. If a single subscription appears with the free trial, it means everything is aligned so that Terraform can eventually create and modify resources under that subscription.

A service principal is typically a dedicated identity that Terraform uses to authenticate programmatically. It is created with a command such as:

```
az ad sp create-for-rbac --role="Contributor" --
scopes="/subscriptions/YOUR_SUBSCRIPTION_ID"
```

The output reveals values like appId, password (clientSecret), and tenant. These correspond to **client_id**, **client_secret**, and **tenant_id** in Terraform's Azure provider configuration. A typical code in Terraform's **main.tf** might look like:

```
provider "azurerm" {
  features {}
  subscription_id = "YOUR_SUBSCRIPTION_ID"
  client_id       = "YOUR_APP_ID"
  client_secret   = "YOUR_CLIENT_SECRET"
  tenant_id       = "YOUR_TENANT_ID"
}
```

The code ensures that Terraform has adequate permissions to create or destroy Azure resources. It should be stressed that storing these secrets in plain text is not ideal for security. Many teams rely on environment variables or secure vaults to hold secrets, referencing them in the provider block with variables.

## Sample Program: Creating Resource Group

A simple way to confirm that the Azure account is fully operational with Terraform is by provisioning a resource group. This is a logical container for Azure resources and represents the basic unit of organization. First, a local folder can be created to store Terraform files, for example **mkdir terraform-azure && cd terraform-azure**. Within that folder, a **main.tf** can be defined with something like:

```
terraform {
  required_providers {
    azurerm = {
      source  = "hashicorp/azurerm"
      version = "=3.0.0"
    }
```

```
  }
}
provider "azurerm" {
  features {}
  subscription_id = var.azure_subscription_id
  client_id       = var.azure_client_id
  client_secret   = var.azure_client_secret
  tenant_id       = var.azure_tenant_id
}
resource "azurerm_resource_group" "example_rg" {
  name     = "example-resource-group"
  location = "EastUS"
}
```

Note that references to **var.azure_*** reflect variables that can be specified in a separate file or as environment variables. An accompanying file named **variables.tf** might look like:

```
variable "azure_subscription_id" {}
variable "azure_client_id" {}
variable "azure_client_secret" {}
variable "azure_tenant_id" {}
```

We then populate those values via a **.tfvars** file or environment variables to avoid storing secrets in the repository. After saving these files, running **terraform init** will download the Azure provider and set up the directory for usage. A follow-up command **terraform plan** shows what will be created, typically listing a single resource group. If everything appears correct, **terraform apply** proceeds to create that group in the specified region. You can verify the resource group's presence in the Azure Portal under Resource Groups. Later, if the resource group is no longer needed, a **terraform destroy** command removes it cleanly. Once a resource group is confirmed, teams can proceed with more complex builds, adding virtual networks, storage, or container services.

# Configure Terraform for Azure

## Provider Configuration and Credential Handling

We are aiming to configure Terraform for Azure typically begin by specifying the Azure provider within a Terraform configuration file. This provider block includes references to necessary credentials such as subscription ID, client ID, client secret, and tenant ID, all of which are linked to a service principal. A minimal setup may look like this:

```
provider "azurerm" {
  features {}
  subscription_id = var.azure_subscription_id
  client_id       = var.azure_client_id
  client_secret   = var.azure_client_secret
  tenant_id       = var.azure_tenant_id
}
```

In the above codes, **`var.azure_*`** placeholders reference variables defined elsewhere, which allows separation of credentials and subscription details from the main code. Storing secrets in environment variables or a **`*.tfvars`** file that remains outside version control is frequently adopted, reducing the risk of leaking sensitive data in a code repository. You can typically run **`terraform init`** afterward to download the Azure provider and confirm connectivity. The default features {} block is required by recent iterations of the azurerm provider, even if no specific features are being customized. Once user has placed correct values in the variable definitions or environment variables, Terraform can authenticate reliably with the Azure subscription. The provider block also supports optional arguments like ARM endpoints for sovereign cloud regions, for instance if the user needs to target Azure US Government or Azure China. In corporate environments, certain policies might require additional role definitions or an explicit scope for the service principal, ensuring that Terraform only manages approved resources in specific resource groups. Teams often find it helpful to verify connectivity by creating a simple resource group, applying the plan, then viewing the result in the Azure Portal.

## Practical Azure Configuration Workflow

Many terraform users prefer to adopt a standard folder layout to keep code manageable. A typical structure might include **`main.tf`** containing the provider block and core resources, **`variables.tf`** defining input variables, and a separate file like **`terraform.tfvars`** for sensitive details. The latter can list subscription_id, client_id, client_secret, and tenant_id under their respective variable names.

For example:

```
variable "azure_subscription_id" {}
variable "azure_client_id" {}
variable "azure_client_secret" {}
variable "azure_tenant_id" {}
```

When **terraform init** is executed within that folder, it detects these variable references and prompts user to provide them unless a tfvars file or environment-based approach is used. If environment variables named TF_VAR_azure_subscription_id or TF_VAR_azure_client_secret exist, Terraform automatically applies their values to the matching variables at runtime. Once initialization is complete, a plan command can illustrate any changes that would occur in the Azure environment. For example, with a resource like azurerm_resource_group, the output might show a single resource to be created. An apply command then calls Azure's APIs to provision that resource. This procedure verifies that the credentials, subscription details, and network connections are correct. If a user sees an authentication error, it is often resolved by confirming that the appId (client_id), password (client_secret), and tenant match the service principal that was created with the az ad sp create-for-rbac command. Occasionally, a user might adjust the Azure Active Directory role assignment if minimal privileges cause Terraform to fail.

# Terraform Commands In-use

Here's a hands-on look at the most commonly used Terraform commands, with some code samples to show how each one's used in a typical workflow. These commands can be used to create, update, inspect, and remove infrastructure resources. We'll use an example Azure configuration to walk through the steps. While the Azure-specific blocks will show up in the code, the core Terraform commands are pretty similar across different cloud providers.

## Sample Project Setup

We often begin by creating a dedicated folder that houses all relevant *.tf files. Let us name it terraform-demo. Within this directory (shown below), one can add the following three files to illustrate a minimal but functional Terraform configuration:

```
terraform-demo/
├── main.tf
├── variables.tf
└── terraform.tfvars
```

The following is an example **main.tf** defining the Azure provider and a single resource group:

```
terraform {
```

```
  required_providers {
    azurerm = {
      source  = "hashicorp/azurerm"
      version = "=3.0.0"
    }
  }
}
provider "azurerm" {
  features {}
  subscription_id = var.azure_subscription_id
  client_id       = var.azure_client_id
  client_secret   = var.azure_client_secret
  tenant_id       = var.azure_tenant_id
}
resource "azurerm_resource_group" "demo_rg" {
  name     = "demo-resource-group"
  location = "EastUS"
}
```

The **variables.tf** might look like this:

```
variable "azure_subscription_id" {}
variable "azure_client_id" {}
variable "azure_client_secret" {}
variable "azure_tenant_id" {}
```

Meanwhile, **terraform.tfvars** stores actual credentials in a secure manner (this file should be ignored by version control):

```
azure_subscription_id = "11111111-2222-3333-4444-555555555555"
azure_client_id       = "abcdef12-3456-7890-abcd-ef1234567890"
azure_client_secret   = "replace_me_with_secure_value"
```

```
azure_tenant_id        = "12345678-abcd-1234-abcd-123456abcdef"
```

With this structure in place, each Terraform command can be demonstrated practically.

## terraform init

We first run **terraform init** in the terraform-demo directory. This command configures the working folder by downloading provider plugins, setting up any declared backend, and verifying the presence of required modules.

```
cd terraform-demo
terraform init
```

When the command runs, Terraform locates the azurerm provider request in **main.tf**. It fetches the provider plugin from the Terraform registry, placing it in a hidden **.terraform** directory. The output usually lists the plugin installation status, followed by a message confirming successful initialization. If a remote backend was defined, **init** would also configure how Terraform stores and manages state outside the local filesystem.

During init, you may see messages indicating which provider versions have been installed and if any module references have been located. If a mismatch arises—perhaps a version higher than specified is requested—**init** warns about version constraints. In this example, we pinned the azurerm provider at "=3.0.0," so Terraform ensures that exact version is downloaded.

## terraform validate

The **terraform validate** command checks the syntax of the *.tf files, ensuring that the HCL is correct and that references to providers, resources, and variables match expected naming conventions.

In the terraform-demo folder, run:

```
terraform validate
```

Terraform scans all configuration files for parseable HCL, proper argument usage, and resource naming. If it detects a misplaced brace, unknown block, or a resource referencing an undefined variable, it returns an error. Otherwise, a success message appears.

Below is a quick sample output you might see:

```
Success! The configuration is valid.
```

A typical reason for failure might be referencing a resource block named **azure_resource_group** when it is actually named **azurerm_resource_group**.

Another possibility involves calling a variable that does not exist. For more complex projects with multiple modules or hundreds of lines of code, a single **terraform validate** helps unify the syntax check, ensuring that no structural problems lurk in any sub-directory.

## terraform fmt

The **terraform fmt** command auto-formats the Terraform files, aligning them with a canonical coding style. You can type:

```
terraform fmt
```

After it runs, Terraform might adjust spacing, indentation, and bracket placement in **main.tf** and other *.tf files. You can check the git diff to confirm these changes. For instance, a line that had inconsistent indentation might now align with Terraform's official styling guidelines. If an entire team uses **terraform fmt** as part of a pre-commit hook, code reviews become smoother since there are fewer whitespace debates or arbitrary formatting differences. Large or nested files, such as those with multiple modules or complex references, benefit significantly from automated formatting. Because consistent style improves readability, new team members can onboard quickly without deciphering arbitrary formatting patterns. You can typically rerun fmt whenever large changes are made to keep everything tidy.

## terraform plan

Once the code is validated and formatted, you can run **terraform plan** to preview which resources will be created, changed, or removed. The plan compares what is in the current state (or empty if no state file exists yet) with what is described in the *.tf configurations:

```
terraform plan
```

Because we are creating a new resource group in Azure, the output typically shows a plus sign (+) next to **azurerm_resource_group.demo_rg**, indicating creation. It might show computed attributes as well, such as an ID that is only known after the resource is created. You carefully review the plan's text to confirm that no unintended actions, like destroying an existing resource group, are present. In more elaborate scenarios, plan might show multiple additions, modifications, or deletions if references or variable values differ from the last time Terraform was run. A color-coded output on terminals usually highlights additions in green, modifications with a tilde, and deletions in red. This visual representation offers clarity about exactly how the environment will change. If user sees unexpected changes—like a resource they never intended to update—it may point to a mismatch in variable definitions or an extraneous block in the code.

Large teams sometimes store the plan output in a file by typing:

```
terraform plan -out=example-plan.out
```

They can then pass that exact file to terraform apply, ensuring no changes creep in between plan and apply steps. This practice is particularly useful in automated pipelines where plans must be approved before deployment.

## terraform apply

We use **`terraform apply`** to execute the changes enumerated in the plan and bring the infrastructure to the desired state. By default, Terraform regenerates the plan, shows it, and prompts for confirmation. If satisfied, typing "yes" commences the provisioning process:

```
terraform apply
```

When the environment is empty, Terraform creates the resource group in Azure. Output on the console displays progress, and if everything succeeds, a final message states that the resources have been added. If one had run **`terraform plan -out=example-plan.out`**, the apply step might be:

```
terraform apply example-plan.out
```

This route guarantees that only the previously reviewed plan is deployed, avoiding any last-minute changes. The process may take seconds or minutes, depending on resource complexity and the responsiveness of the Azure API. If any error occurs—like invalid credentials or insufficient permissions—Terraform halts and logs the details. Resolving that issue and re-running apply typically picks up where it left off, except for resources that might need partial rollback. After success, you can often check the Azure Portal or use the Azure CLI to confirm that "demo-resource-group" now exists in the correct location. Terraform also updates the local or remote state so that future plans reflect the newly provisioned environment.

## terraform show

The **`terraform show`** command lets yo check the current state. It reveals each resource that Terraform manages, along with property values known to the system. In the terraform-demo directory, running:

```
terraform show
```

outputs a detailed breakdown of the resource group's attributes, such as its ID in Azure, name, location, and tags. If more resources exist—like virtual networks, subnets, or storage accounts—the listing extends to those as well. Because the show command enumerates everything in state, it can be quite verbose. You might pipe the output to grep or less to filter for relevant lines. In advanced cases, they may use **`terraform state show <resource>`** to isolate a specific resource. This direct inquiry is useful for debugging or referencing dynamically generated values in other HCL expressions. For instance, if the user has an output block that exposes a resource group's ID, they can compare it against what show prints to see if it aligns with expectations.

## terraform destroy

For ephemeral environments or test deployments, you may remove infrastructure once it is no longer required, saving costs and keeping environments clean. The **`terraform destroy`** command systematically tears down every resource from the current configuration state:

```
terraform destroy
```

Terraform displays a plan listing which resources will be destroyed, typically the same ones that were created by apply. After prompting for confirmation, it calls the Azure APIs to delete them. A color-coded output shows each resource as it is removed, and once finished, the state is updated to reflect that nothing is left under management.

# HashiCorp Configuration Language (HCL)

## Design Philosophy

HCL was created with the goal of balancing machine readability with human-friendliness, unlike many configuration languages that tend to be rigid or overly verbose. The emphasis on human readability makes code reviews and collaboration more natural, while the strict structure still lends itself to reliable machine parsing and error detection. HCL's syntax relies on nested blocks that combine keys, values, and expressions to describe resources, providers, variables, outputs, and any other configuration element. Each block typically begins with a keyword and an optional label, followed by a set of braces that contain arguments or nested blocks. This approach brings a degree of organization that is intuitive who deal with multiple resources in large-scale infrastructures. At the same time, it preserves enough flexibility to adapt to the complex relationships and dependencies that often arise when building environments across multiple providers or in multi-cloud setups.

Another advantage is that HCL is internally consistent across different HashiCorp tools, which reduces the learning curve for those who use Vault, Consul, or other products from the same ecosystem. It is also JSON compatible, so teams can switch to JSON format when automation or programmatic generation of configuration files is preferred, while still preserving the clarity offered by a nested, block-oriented structure. The design aim of keeping HCL approachable for humans makes it practical for day-to-day tasks while empowering teams to treat infrastructure definitions as living documentation, bridging the gap between developers, operations engineers, and anyone else who needs to understand how resources are being allocated and configured.

## Blocks, Arguments, and Expressions

HCL leverages blocks, arguments, and expressions as its primary building blocks, allowing configurations to be both readable and modular. A block is introduced by a resource type or keyword, followed by a name or label, and then enclosed in curly braces. Within these braces, arguments define attributes. Arguments are formatted as key-value pairs, capturing the specific properties of a resource or provider. For example, a resource block might appear as:

```
resource "azurerm_virtual_network" "example_vnet" {
  name                = "exampleVnet"
  location            =
azurerm_resource_group.example_rg.location
  resource_group_name = azurerm_resource_group.example_rg.name
  address_space       = ["10.0.0.0/16"]
}
```

The block type here is resource, the resource name is **azurerm_virtual_network**, and the local label is example_vnet, which references this block elsewhere in the code. The body includes arguments like name, location, **resource_group_name**, and **address_space**. Check expressions—such as **azurerm_resource_group.example_rg.location**—reference attributes from other blocks, enabling inter-resource relationships without duplicated data. This referencing approach fosters consistency while reducing the risk of spelling mistakes or mismatched resource properties. HCL also supports nested blocks within resource blocks, enabling more complex behaviors or multiple sub-resources tied to the primary resource. For instance, a storage container could have one or more nested blocks for container access policies, each block specifying additional arguments. These hierarchical relationships reduce complexity by logically grouping configurations and preventing random scattering of properties. This is particularly useful in advanced scenarios with complex dependencies. HCL's expression syntax goes beyond referencing other blocks, offering function calls, conditionals, and for expressions that let you dynamically define attributes, iterate over maps or lists, and generate multiple nested blocks based on variable inputs.

## Variables, Outputs, and Data Structures

Variables and outputs are first-class concepts in HCL that encourage modular, reusable code while keeping sensitive or environment-specific data out of the main configuration. Variables are declared with a variable block specifying a name and optional constraints like type or default value. You can pass their actual values at runtime through a **.tfvars** file, environment variables, or interactive prompts.

For example:

```
variable "instance_size" {
```

```
  type    = string
  default = "Standard_DS1_v2"
}
```

This declares a variable named instance_size, which might be used when defining a virtual machine resource. You can override the default by specifying a different value in a **.tfvars** file or passing **-var "instance_size=Standard_DS2_v2"** at the command line.

Outputs, on the other hand, are a mechanism for exposing resource attributes, computed values, or references to other systems. One can define an output named instance_ip that references a virtual machine's primary public IP, making it simple to retrieve or display after a successful terraform apply. Data structures like lists, maps, and objects also enrich the expressiveness of HCL. Lists might define subnets or a set of availability zones, while maps can store key-value pairs of tags or region-specific settings.

Conditionals and for expressions take this a step further, supporting advanced logic that merges or filters data sets during runtime. HCL remains strongly typed, so a user who tries to assign a string to a list variable or pass an integer where a boolean is expected encounters a clear error during validation or planning. This strong typing, combined with consistent block syntax, helps ensure that configurations remain coherent and straightforward to maintain, even as the underlying infrastructure evolves over time.

# My First Terraform Configuration

## Project Layout and File Creation

A practical way to learn HCL and Terraform is by creating a small project that manages a real cloud resource. You can simply create a folder on the local workstation where all Terraform configuration files reside. Let us name it **my-first-terraform-config**. Inside this directory, multiple *.tf files can be placed.

For the simplest demonstration, one can start with a single **main.tf** that contains everything. However, as a project grows, it is better to introduce separate files for variables, outputs, and modules.

Below is a minimal structure to get started:

```
my-first-terraform-config/
 ├── main.tf
 └── variables.tf
```

In **main.tf**, declare the provider and a small resource, such as an Azure resource group or an

AWS S3 bucket, depending on the target platform. For Azure, a block might look like:

```
terraform {
  required_providers {
    azurerm = {
      source  = "hashicorp/azurerm"
      version = "=3.0.0"
    }
  }
}
provider "azurerm" {
  features {}
  subscription_id = var.azure_subscription_id
  client_id       = var.azure_client_id
  client_secret   = var.azure_client_secret
  tenant_id       = var.azure_tenant_id
}
resource "azurerm_resource_group" "hello_rg" {
  name     = "myFirstRG"
  location = "EastUS"
}
```

This above program introduces the provider block for Azure, referencing local variables for credentials, which you then define in **variables.tf**. The resource block declares an azurerm_resource_group named hello_rg, with a name of "myFirstRG" and a location set to "EastUS." The resource group is typically the foundational container in Azure for any subsequent resources. By explicitly referencing **var.azure_*** placeholders, you encourage secure separation of secrets from the main code. Meanwhile, the call to version = "=3.0.0" ensures that the code runs with a consistent provider release. After creating these files, the directory is prepared for initialization, planning, and application using Terraform commands.

## Sample Variables and Credentials

Within **variables.tf**, define the variables that were referenced in the provider block:

```
variable "azure_subscription_id" {}
variable "azure_client_id" {}
variable "azure_client_secret" {}
variable "azure_tenant_id" {}
```

We can then specify the actual values in a **.tfvars** file named **terraform.tfvars** or rely on environment variables named TF_VAR_azure_subscription_id, TF_VAR_azure_client_id, etc. An example **terraform.tfvars** might look like:

```
azure_subscription_id = "11111111-2222-3333-4444-555555555555"
azure_client_id       = "aaaaaaaa-bbbb-cccc-dddd-eeeeeeeeeeee"
azure_client_secret   = "paste_secret_here"
azure_tenant_id       = "99999999-1111-2222-3333-444444444444"
```

This approach prevents exposure of credentials in version control if **terraform.tfvars** is added to .gitignore or similar. Once these pieces are in place, a user can open a terminal within the project folder and run **terraform init**. Terraform downloads the azurerm provider if not already present, then sets up the local environment. A typical next step is **terraform plan**, which compares the desired configuration to the current empty state and indicates that one resource (the resource group) will be created. After reviewing, a user applies the changes with **terraform apply**, confirming "yes" to proceed. Terraform orchestrates an API call to Azure, creating the resource group. When the process completes, a user can check the Azure Portal to confirm that "myFirstRG" now exists in the "EastUS" region.

## Adding Virtual Network/Resource

The real power of Terraform becomes more evident when layering additional resources. In the same **main.tf**, a user might add a block for an Azure Virtual Network:

```
resource "azurerm_virtual_network" "hello_vnet" {
  name                = "myFirstVNet"
  location            =
azurerm_resource_group.hello_rg.location
  resource_group_name = azurerm_resource_group.hello_rg.name
  address_space       = ["10.0.0.0/16"]
}
```

You need to check that location and resource_group_name reference attributes from the hello_rg resource. This reference ensures if you rename the resource group, or if you move it to another region, the virtual network automatically follows those changes without requiring manual updates. A fresh plan shows that Terraform wants to add the new network as well. After applying, you can see both the resource group and the virtual network in the Azure Portal. This pattern scales: subsequent code blocks might define subnets, network security groups, or even a virtual machine. Each block uses references to previously declared resources to ensure consistent relationships and reduce repetition. By systematically adding resources, you can build up entire architectures while preserving clarity in HCL. If something does not work as expected, running **`terraform show`** or investigating plan output clarifies what Terraform thinks the environment should look like and reveals any mismatch between the code and reality.

## Testing and Cleaning Up

After confirming that everything is functioning, you can tear down the environment with a single command:

```
terraform destroy
```

This systematically removes the resource group, the virtual network, and anything else that was created in the configuration. The command displays a plan that marks each item for destruction, prompting for confirmation. If user wants a fresh environment, the same apply command can be re-run, re-provisioning all declared resources.

# Executing Terraform Configuration

## Initializing, Validating and Planning

We often store their Terraform definitions in a dedicated folder, containing files such as **`main.tf`**, **`variables.tf`**, and possibly a **`terraform.tfvars`** for credentials or sensitive data. To begin, open a command-line interface in that folder and run:

```
terraform init
```

This command locates any provider specifications in the configuration files, downloads the corresponding plugins, and prepares the environment to handle the defined infrastructure. A typical scenario might include the azurerm provider for Azure or one of the providers for AWS, Google Cloud, or VMware. Once **`init`** completes, **`.terraform`** directory appears, listing the downloaded provider binaries and any required modules. Another step involves checking the syntax and structural validity of the configuration:

```
terraform validate
```

An output indicating success means the configuration is correctly structured. If a variable or resource is misspelled, or if HCL syntax is broken, the process aborts with a descriptive message. You then produce a preview of planned actions:

```
terraform plan
```

This command compares the local code against the state file (if one exists) and generates a list of additions, modifications, or deletions needed to match the desired infrastructure. In a new project with no existing resources, plan might show multiple items marked with a plus sign (+), confirming creation. You review the plan to confirm resource details align with expectations. The plan also includes attribute references, such as an auto-generated name or an ID that will appear upon creation. Large projects generate a lengthy plan output, which can be saved to a file by appending the -out parameter:

```
terraform plan -out=myplan.out
```

Such an approach is often used in collaborative settings where team members review the plan in a version control system or a continuous integration pipeline. Once satisfied, you can proceed with apply, referencing the same plan file.

## Applying Deployment

The phase of applying the planned configuration is initiated with:

```
terraform apply
```

When the plan was not saved to a file beforehand, Terraform recalculates the plan, displays a summary of expected changes, and prompts for user confirmation. Typing yes finalizes the process, triggering Terraform to connect with the cloud provider and create the resources declared in the code. For instance, if **main.tf** references an Azure Resource Group named "ProjectRG" in "WestUS," the console logs each creation step as the provider responds.

Following is a quick example defining such a group:

```
resource "azurerm_resource_group" "project_rg" {
  name     = "ProjectRG"
  location = "WestUS"
}
```

During apply, a typical message might read:

```
azurerm_resource_group.project_rg:
Creating...
```

followed by the completion statement that includes an ID or other relevant data. Once the operation finishes, Terraform updates the local or remote state file to reflect that the resource group now exists, preventing re-creation in future plan commands. You can then check the associated portal—such as the Azure Portal—for confirmation. If a resource fails to create due to permission or configuration issues, Terraform halts with an error. A fix can be applied to the code or credentials, followed by another apply to complete partially created infrastructure. Incremental modifications proceed similarly, using plan to preview changes, then apply to enact them. For instance, if user adds a virtual network resource referencing the newly created resource group, a subsequent plan might show a new + entry. After verifying the details, an apply introduces that network into the environment.

# Destroy Resources with Terraform

When resources are no longer needed, or if a temporary testing environment has served its purpose, Terraform removes them through the destroy command as below:

```
terraform destroy
```

Terraform reads the current state file, enumerates every resource it manages, and proposes a plan marking each resource for deletion. This plan is displayed much like in the apply process, showing a minus sign (-) beside each resource and attribute as below:

```
- azurerm_resource_group.project_rg will be destroyed
  ...
Plan: 0 to add, 0 to change, 1 to destroy.
```

This indicates that the project_rg resource is about to be permanently deleted, along with all associated data or objects the provider automatically cleans up. If a resource is missing from the configuration but still present in the provider's environment, Terraform may not list it for destruction unless it was imported or tracked.

# Summary

So, we dug into the nitty-gritty of what Terraform can do. First, we got the hang of installing and setting up Terraform on a Linux machine, and then we prepared Microsoft Azure for Terraform setups. Setting up Terraform is pretty straightforward. You just download the necessary Terraform package for the system, extract the package, and add the Terraform binary to the

PATH environment variable of the system.

After that, we covered some of the basic commands and features of the Terraform CLI. We went over some of the main commands, like init, plan, apply, and destroy, which are super important for managing Terraform resources. We also learned about the HCL and how it assists us to build and manage resources in a declarative way, meaning we just have to say what we want, and Terraform will handle the rest. Finally, we got our hands dirty with Terraform by writing, applying, and then trashing our very first Terraform configuration.

# Chapter 3: Essentials of Terraform Configuration Language

# Variables Definitions

## Characteristics of Variables

A person looking to craft flexible Terraform configurations often relies on variables to inject external values without editing the underlying code each time a change is required. Variables serve as placeholders which you can customize, enabling the same configuration to behave differently across environments such as development, testing, or production. The ability to parameterize infrastructure code eliminates hard-coded constants and encourages more reusable, maintainable setups. When a Terraform configuration contains resource blocks that reference these variables, Terraform replaces each variable reference with the real-world value provided at runtime, whether from a file, environment variable, or command-line option. This behavior allows you to scale or alter infrastructure details simply by adjusting variable data, rather than duplicating entire configuration files for each slight modification.

Variables also enhance collaboration because different individuals or teams can work on the same codebase while applying unique values for particular deployments. That scenario is valuable in large organizations managing multiple accounts, clouds, or data centers. By using variables, code remains consistent, easy to read, and relatively abstracted from environment-specific nuances. There is also an opportunity to add descriptive fields (such as the description argument in a variable block) so future users can understand the intended usage, acceptable input types, and default values of each variable.

## Declaring Input Variables

A typical Terraform configuration organizes variable blocks in a dedicated file named **`variables.tf`**. Each variable block starts with the keyword variable followed by a quoted identifier. Inside the block, arguments such as type, default, and description may appear as below:

```
variable "location" {
  type        = string
  description = "Geographical location for resources"
  default     = "EastUS"
}
```

In the above, location is declared as a string with a default value. If no override is provided at runtime, "EastUS" is used. When referencing this variable in a resource, you may typically use var.location, as in:

```
resource "azurerm_resource_group" "rg" {
```

```
  name     = "demo-resource-group"
  location = var.location
}
```

That approach ensures the code remains generic. You can override location from a **terraform.tfvars** file, environment variables prefixed by TF_VAR_, or a -var argument on the command line. A typical tfvars file might contain location = "WestUS" to switch the region. Such a design pattern is convenient because one can quickly change multiple aspects of an environment by editing a single file, rather than combing through multiple resource definitions.

## Advanced Variable Types and Validation

We often discover that variables can handle more complex data structures, including lists, maps, and objects. This ability is extremely practical when code must define repeated properties or dynamic resource counts.

For example, the user might define a list of instance sizes:

```
variable "instance_sizes" {
  type        = list(string)
  description = "Allowed sizes for virtual machines in the
cluster"
  default     = ["Standard_DS1_v2", "Standard_DS2_v2"]
}
```

Elsewhere in the code, one might iterate over that list with a for_each or count meta-argument, provisioning multiple resources based on each value. Meanwhile, a map can store key-value associations, such as environment to domain mappings or data center region codes.

Objects go a step further, bundling together properties in a structured manner. A variable block for an object might define multiple fields, each with its own type, enabling the user to pass a single variable containing multiple related settings. In addition, starting with certain Terraform versions, a validation block can be used to impose constraints on input values. The user might require that a list is not empty or that a numeric variable stays within a certain range, returning a readable error if the input fails these checks. This technique ensures that incorrect usage of the configuration is caught early, preventing partially configured resources from being deployed.

## Sample Program: Combining Variables

A practical configuration often includes multiple variables working together to define a cloud environment. Suppose the user wants to parameterize both the resource group location and the number of virtual machines to create. To do this, we might do it as below:

```
variable "location" {
  type        = string
  description = "Geographical location for resources"
  default     = "EastUS"
}
variable "vm_count" {
  type        = number
  description = "Number of virtual machines to create"
  default     = 2
}
```

In **main.tf**, these appear:

```
resource "azurerm_resource_group" "main_rg" {
  name     = "multi-vm-demo"
  location = var.location
}
resource "azurerm_virtual_machine" "demo_vms" {
  count               = var.vm_count
  name                = "demo-vm-${count.index}"
  location            =
azurerm_resource_group.main_rg.location
  resource_group_name = azurerm_resource_group.main_rg.name
  # Additional VM configuration...
}
```

When the user runs terraform plan, the code sees vm_count is 2, so it proposes creation of two virtual machines named "demo-vm-0" and "demo-vm-1." The variable location sets the region for both the resource group and the machines. If a team wants three VMs in "WestUS," they update the tfvars or pass -var "vm_count=3" -var "location=WestUS" at runtime. The user can store these values in a version-controlled tfvars file, an environment variable, or pass them via CLI arguments.

# Interpolation Syntax

## Concept of Interpolation

Terraform's interpolation syntax is a mechanism for dynamically inserting values or expressions into configuration blocks. The hallmark is the notation ${}, which encloses references to variables, resource attributes, or function calls. Interpolation is an integral part of how Terraform composes final configurations from modular and parametric definitions. It lets one reference attributes from other resources, pass data between modules, and conditionally compute property values in response to user inputs. In older Terraform versions, the interpolation syntax was essential for all references. Modern versions allow referencing expressions without braces when they are used as standalone values, but certain complex expressions still rely on the original bracketed notation. For example, referencing var.name is valid in many contexts, yet advanced usage such as string concatenation often looks like "my-prefix-${var.name}". Users who adopt these dynamic expressions can keep configurations more flexible and avoid repeating known data such as region codes, IP addresses, or resource IDs.

Interpolation also makes straightforward to produce computed fields, like generating a unique name suffix for each environment or deriving a resource name from multiple variables. By mixing string literals with references to resource attributes or built-in functions, the code can adapt to shifting requirements without any manual renaming or duplication. This way, it fosters a single configuration that stands the test of time, as any underlying resource detail changes only once while all related references adapt seamlessly.

## Simple Interpolation vs. Complex Expressions

A basic interpolation might be as simple as referencing a variable within a resource argument, such as:

```
name = "${var.instance_name}"
```

However, as of Terraform 1.0 and above, many simpler references can omit the ${} braces and simply write name = var.instance_name. The bracketed syntax still appears when you need to concatenate strings or embed references within text. For instance, "demo-${var.instance_name}-vm" splices var.instance_name in the middle of a literal, ensuring that the final value is computed at runtime based on user input or environment data.

Suppose the user wants to transform a user-supplied string to uppercase or compute the length of a list. One could embed "prefix-${upper(var.env_name)}" or use length(var.subnet_list) to dynamically compute aspects of a resource configuration. Another pattern involves referencing attributes from other resources as below:

```
resource "aws_subnet" "main_subnet" {
```

```
  vpc_id = var.vpc_id
  cidr_block = "${cidrsubnet(var.vpc_cidr, 2, 1)}"
}
resource "aws_instance" "app_server" {
  subnet_id = aws_subnet.main_subnet.id
  # ...
}
```

Here, the instance depends on the subnet's ID, while the subnet itself references a function call generating a new subnet range from var.vpc_cidr. Interpolation ties these references together, ensuring the correct order of creation and guaranteeing that updates cascade. Without interpolation, each resource would require manual entry of data that might quickly diverge from reality if changed in one place but not another.

## Functions, Conditionals, and Built-In Operators

Expressions do more than reference variables or resource attributes; they can also invoke built-in functions. The repertoire includes string manipulation (like trim, lower, upper, substring), numeric operations (max, min, abs), cryptographic hashing (md5, sha256), and more. Conditional logic is also present to define properties that vary based on environment constraints.

For example, a resource could set a count to var.num_instances if var.env_type == "prod", or zero if not. Terraform uses a ternary-like syntax: condition ? true_val : false_val:

```
count = var.env_type == "prod" ? 3 : 1
```

Another scenario might involve using the coalesce function to pick the first non-null input from a list of values. The ability to chain such functions within an interpolation block fosters a dynamic style that can adapt to ephemeral data or shifting user preferences. However, best practices warn against turning Terraform configurations into overly complex "mini-programs." Overusing complicated expressions can hamper readability. The recommended approach is to keep expressions relatively straightforward, relying on modules or external scripts if heavy logic is needed.

## Sample Program: Interpolation in Action

Let's say you want to create a naming pattern that includes environment details. You could make a variable called env_name set to "staging." You could define it like this:

```
resource "azurerm_virtual_machine" "vm" {
```

```
  name                = "myapp-${var.env_name}-vm"
  location            = var.location
  resource_group_name = azurerm_resource_group.rg.name
  # ...
}
```

When the code runs, the VM name becomes "myapp-staging-vm." If user sets var.env_name to "prod," that same line transforms into "myapp-prod-vm."

Another example is referencing an output from a separate resource, as with:

```
resource "random_id" "rand" {
  byte_length = 4
}
resource "azurerm_storage_account" "sa" {
  name                = "storageacct${random_id.rand.hex}"
  location            = var.location
  resource_group_name = azurerm_resource_group.rg.name
  # ...
}
```

In the above, the storage account name is computed by appending the hex value from random_id.rand. Another user might define a function-based expression to pick the correct region from a map based on environment type. That map might appear as var.region_map = { dev = "EastUS", prod = "WestUS" }, while the assignment uses var.region_map[var.env_type] to retrieve the correct location.

# Conditional Expressions

Terraform configurations sometimes call for different behaviors or resource attributes depending on user inputs or environment settings, and conditional expressions enable a single codebase to handle these varied conditions seamlessly. The syntax condition ? true_val : false_val returns one of two values, determined by whether the boolean condition is met. The user might use conditionals to decide how many instances to deploy based on environment type, or whether to enable a specific feature for only certain environments.

I'll give you an example. Say we have a code snippet that shows this approach. It might declare a variable named environment, defaulted to "dev," and rely on a resource block that uses a conditional for the count as below:

```
variable "environment" {
  type    = string
  default = "dev"
}
resource "aws_instance" "demo" {
  count = var.environment == "prod" ? 3 : 1
  # ...
}
```

When environment is "prod," Terraform provisions three instances, otherwise it creates only one. This design pattern keeps the configuration flexible and prevents code repetition. It is also common to see conditionals used in resource properties themselves, such as instance sizes or optional fields. For example, the user might declare a boolean variable named enable_logging, then apply a conditional expression to pick a more powerful instance if logging is enabled, or a smaller instance if not. That snippet may appear as instance_type = var.enable_logging ? "t2.medium" : "t2.micro". The primary benefit is that you do not have to rewrite entire blocks for multiple cases; rather, each scenario is determined by simple logic, leading to a more concise and modular configuration.

Conditional expressions can also nest, though it is wise to keep them at a manageable level for readability. An overly nested chain of conditionals can cause confusion, so you can commonly rely on maps or external logic for more complex branching. Another technique is to combine conditionals with other interpolation features, such as referencing resource attributes, to enable advanced scenario handling. For example, count could be set to var.some_toggle && local.some_condition ? 2 : 0, mixing boolean expressions with local values. This ensures that the resource either appears twice or not at all, depending on environment constraints.

# Loops and Dynamic Blocks

Terraform offers robust looping capabilities so that repetitive resource definitions or sub-blocks can be generated from lists, maps, or sets. The count meta-argument is a straightforward option when the objective is to create a specified number of similar resources. A variable such as vm_count might default to 2, while setting count = var.vm_count in a resource block instructs Terraform to produce that many copies. You can differentiate each copy using the count.index value, for example naming resources as "vm-${count.index}" or referencing them individually within the state file. This approach reduces code duplication while making expansions or contractions easy—just update the variable, re-run plan, and observe how Terraform calculates additions or removals.

Meanwhile, for_each is better suited when resource creation depends on a map or set of strings, so each resource can be keyed by a unique identifier. Suppose the user has a map named var.instances = { "web" = "t2.micro", "db" = "t2.small" }. By specifying for_each = var.instances, each resource is labeled with the key "web" or "db," and each.value references the instance size. The result is two resources that differ by name and size but share the same base configuration block. This design fosters a parametric style, letting the code scale or adapt simply by adjusting the map in **`variables.tf`** or a **`.tfvars`** file.

Dynamic blocks extend this concept to sub-blocks within a resource. A frequent example is a security group that includes multiple ingress or egress rules. Instead of writing out each rule individually, a dynamic "ingress" block with a for_each loops over a list of rule objects. Each iteration sets attributes like from_port, to_port, and cidr_blocks based on the current element.

Following is a quick example:

```
variable "ingress_rules" {
  type = list(object({
    from_port   = number
    to_port     = number
    protocol    = string
    cidr_blocks = list(string)
  }))
  default = [
    { from_port = 22, to_port = 22, protocol = "tcp",
cidr_blocks = ["0.0.0.0/0"] },
    { from_port = 80, to_port = 80, protocol = "tcp",
cidr_blocks = ["0.0.0.0/0"] }
  ]
}
resource "aws_security_group" "demo_sg" {
  name   = "demoSG"
  vpc_id = var.vpc_id
  dynamic "ingress" {
    for_each = var.ingress_rules
```

```
    content {
      from_port   = ingress.value.from_port
      to_port     = ingress.value.to_port
      protocol    = ingress.value.protocol
      cidr_blocks = ingress.value.cidr_blocks
    }
  }
}
```

This approach spares the user from copying and pasting multiple blocks, which can introduce errors or become unwieldy if numerous rules exist. Changing or adding a rule simply involves updating var.ingress_rules. Terraform then adjusts the plan accordingly, adding or modifying the relevant sub-block. Similar logic applies to outputs, nested resource definitions, and provisioning scripts. Many users also leverage local values or modules to keep looping logic encapsulated, preventing the main configuration from getting cluttered.

# Summary

As we went through this chapter, we really dived into the ins and outs of the configuration language that Terraform uses. We knew that variables were a huge part of HCL because they let users tweak their settings to fit their needs, and we knew how to make the most of these variables. As we kept exploring HCL, we came across conditional expressions, which let you set values based on conditions. We also discovered that these expressions are very powerful when combined with Terraform's loop constructions, specifically count and for_each, and that this is one of the reasons for their popularity. We showed how simple it is to generate numerous copies of a resource by using the count function.

Finally, we checked out Terraform's dynamic blocks, which add to the expressiveness of HCL's nature while also making it more dynamic. This construct makes it possible to specify several similar blocks within a resource based on complex types such as lists or maps, which is a skill that is particularly valuable when working with larger and more sophisticated configurations.

# Chapter 4: Terraform Modules and Reusable Infrastructure

# Introduction to Reusable Infrastructure

Infrastructure creation and management often involve repetitive patterns that recur across projects, teams, or entire organizations. Many discover that a new application or environment usually requires the same kinds of resources, like virtual networks, security rules, and compute instances, albeit with small variations. This method integrates well with an IaC philosophy, where cloud or on-premises resources are defined in machine-readable files. When these definitions are written once and proven, they can be applied repeatedly with different parameters, allowing for rapid scaling, consistent settings, and straightforward maintenance. You then spend less time configuring the same fundamentals over and over. They focus instead on higher-value tasks, like refining an application or ensuring robust security. This approach also allows new contributors to ramp up quicker, since they can reference a known code blueprint rather than figuring out an entire environment from scratch.

A real perspective on reusable infrastructure recognizes that each environment can share building blocks such as standardized images, naming conventions, or network topologies. One example is the concept of a standard "web front-end stack," which might include load balancers, firewall rules, and a cluster of virtual machines. By writing a single set of definitions for this front-end stack, teams can apply it to any new product line or test environment simply by adjusting a few inputs. This cuts down on the overhead of writing new resource definitions, verifying them, and debugging subtle differences. Another key motivation is cost optimization: if every environment references the same blueprint, you can measure and predict resource usage more accurately, quickly spotting anomalies when usage spikes or drops unexpectedly. That level of transparency benefits capacity planning, because the same pattern is reused enough times that its operational profile is well understood.

Reusable infrastructure also reduces the worry of configuration drift, where multiple environments gradually diverge from their initial state. If every environment is derived from a single code library of modules or templates, updates and improvements can be rolled out systematically rather than patched manually. This uniformity simplifies compliance checks, since environments are no longer one-off creations with potential misconfigurations. Security specialists, for instance, can embed best practices directly into these reusable definitions, ensuring the entire organization benefits immediately. Additionally, staff can rely on version-controlled changes so that if an improvement inadvertently breaks an environment, it is easy to revert to a known stable definition. When each environment can be traced to the same building block, teams are better positioned to track performance metrics, diagnose issues, and provide consistent support to internal or external users.

A real-world illustration might involve a large company that needs multiple staging environments with identical load balancing, subnets, and logs. Rather than building each environment from scratch, engineers can reference the same blueprint or module. They override variables such as environment name or instance size to fit the staging needs. Should the central team refine the logging solution or patch a vulnerability, that fix can be pushed into the shared code, ensuring every derived environment stays aligned. If local customizations exist, they become small deltas on top of the standard blueprint, which is far easier to track than having entirely custom code for each environment. This focus on shared references prevents an explosion of ephemeral, hand-crafted solutions that nobody fully understands a few months later.

Reusable infrastructure ultimately shortens lead times. They quickly replicate proven architectures that match production-grade standards. They also gain confidence that a newly launched environment is stable, because it is the same fundamental structure used a dozen times before. Even post-deployment, uniform infrastructure is simpler to monitor and troubleshoot. For instance, if a developer sees a certain pattern of CPU usage on one environment, they can trust that the same pattern likely holds for others. This consistency fosters knowledge sharing, fosters a collaborative mindset, and reduces friction in day-to-day operations.

# Terraform Modules

Terraform modules present a structured approach to implementing reusable infrastructure patterns. Each module packages a set of Terraform configurations into a logical unit that can be invoked from elsewhere. A module might define the resources for a microservice stack, including its network, instances, and security rules. By giving modules parameters, you can tailor the resources to the needs of each environment while reusing the code.

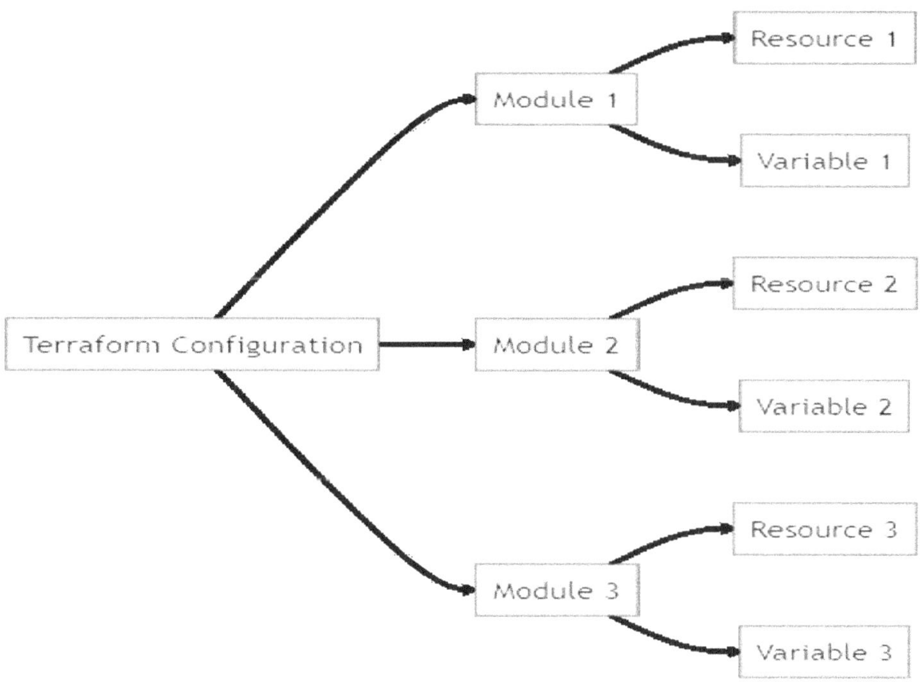


**Fig 4.1 Concept of Terraform Modules**

Below is an example demonstrating a module that configures a simple Azure Virtual Network. The directory structure could look like this:

```
modules/
 azure_vnet/
   main.tf
   variables.tf
   outputs.tf
```

Inside **variables.tf**, the developer might declare inputs:

```
variable "resource_group_name" {
  type        = string
  description = "Name of the resource group"
}
variable "location" {
  type        = string
  description = "Azure region for resources"
}
variable "vnet_name" {
  type        = string
  description = "Name of the virtual network"
}
variable "address_space" {
  type        = list(string)
  default     = ["10.0.0.0/16"]
}
```

In **main.tf**, the module creates a VNet:

```
resource "azurerm_virtual_network" "demo_vnet" {
  name                = var.vnet_name
  resource_group_name = var.resource_group_name
```

```
  location             = var.location
  address_space        = var.address_space
}
```

Finally, **outputs.tf** reveals important information:

```
output "vnet_id" {
  description = "ID of the created virtual network"
  value       = azurerm_virtual_network.demo_vnet.id
}
```

Another Terraform configuration can call this module by referencing the path or a source control URL:

```
module "my_vnet" {
  source              = "./modules/azure_vnet"
  resource_group_name = "shared-resources"
  location            = "EastUS"
  vnet_name           = "vnet-production"
}
```

This call spares user from rewriting the VNet resource repeatedly, while letting them adjust location, name, or address space for each environment.

Modules become especially valuable when layered. A larger module can reference smaller submodules that each handle a slice of functionality (e.g. subnets, security rules, or route tables). For instance, the main **azure_infra** module might define an Azure resource group, then call a **vnet** submodule to handle the network, and a **subnet** submodule to set up each subnet. Each submodule can be updated independently, pinned to a particular version, and tested in isolation. That pattern avoids overwhelming a single file with hundreds of resource definitions. It also fosters collaboration: different teams might maintain submodules specialized to a function like monitoring or data warehousing. If a resource definition changes (for instance, a new tagging policy or added encryption setting), the updated submodule can be rolled out systematically across all referencing modules.

Plus, versioning makes sure you can count on using the same modules from one version to the next. If the module is hosted on GitHub or in a private registry, a user can specify a particular version tag to avoid surprises.

For example,

```
source = "git::https://github.com/org/azure_vnet?ref=v1.2.0"
```

means the environment always uses the code from the 1.2.0 tag. Some teams adopt semantic versioning so that bug fixes increment the patch number, minor additions increment the middle number, and major changes that might break compatibility increment the first number.

There's a typical way to build modules that includes a short README that describes how to use the module, what the inputs and outputs are, and some example calls. If someone wants to use the module, they can check the README to see exactly what inputs are needed and what the module returns. If the user runs **`terraform plan`** after referencing the module, Terraform fetches the module definitions from the specified source, merges them into the plan, and prompts for any missing variables. The result is a consistent, maintainable approach to spinning up resources. Organizations frequently keep a repository or registry of modules for common tasks like networking, load balancers, or container orchestration.

Nested modules represent a further level of composability, allowing one module to call another. This practice might group all network resources into a single directory, but internally, the module references submodules for VNet, subnets, and network security groups. That hierarchy aligns with how large infrastructures scale. Each submodule is smaller, more focused, and simpler to maintain, while the parent module orchestrates them to create a coherent environment. The final calling code—often in a root directory—just references the parent module, abstracting away the complexities. This style ensures that the code is both modular and flexible, letting you expand or refactor the architecture without rewriting everything. If a new environment requires an extra subnet, it can be added by adjusting variables in the parent module, which then orchestrates the submodules to produce the updated infrastructure plan.

# Module Inputs

A large number of practitioners rely on module inputs to convert Terraform modules into flexible, adaptable building blocks. When modules accept parameters, teams can adjust resource configurations without modifying the underlying code, leading to consistent yet customizable infrastructure patterns. Suppose a module establishes a virtual machine, security group, or network. By defining input variables in the module, such as instance size, location, or tags, individuals referencing that module can supply environment-specific values at runtime. This dramatically reduces the need to duplicate large sections of configuration for each environment or project. It also preserves a single code path where new features or corrections can be introduced once and then adopted by all modules' consumers. For instance, a module dedicated to deploying an Azure Virtual Network may have variables named resource_group_name, location, and address_space. When a user needs another network in a different region, they pass a distinct location value into the same module. This approach helps unify the style of resource creation, fosters collaboration between multiple teams, and lowers error rates.

Moreover, variables can carry built-in validation rules or type constraints (like string, number, or list) that prevent invalid usage. Following is a simple example that shows how to define and invoke module inputs:

```
# Inside a module's variables.tf
variable "resource_group_name" {
  type        = string
  description = "Name of the resource group for all resources"
}
variable "location" {
  type        = string
  description = "Azure region where resources are deployed"
}
variable "vnet_name" {
  type        = string
  description = "Azure Virtual Network name"
  default     = "default-vnet"
}
# Calling the module from a root configuration
module "my_vnet" {
  source              = "./modules/azure_vnet"
  resource_group_name = "rg-shared"
  location            = "WestEurope"
  vnet_name           = "internal-network"
}
```

At first, the module sets up variables for critical parameters, including a default for vnet_name. And later, it references the module with different values. This design pattern accelerates environment provisioning because each user or automation pipeline needs only to supply relevant data, skipping the effort of rewriting the Terraform logic for every new deployment.

# Module Locals

Many developers employ local values to encapsulate internal computations or expressions within a module, creating a tidy space where repeated logic is defined only once. Locals can be thought of as named constants or computed results that remain hidden from module consumers. When a project needs a unique naming scheme, merges multiple lists or maps, or calculates a final value from several inputs, writing the expression in multiple places can lead to errors and clutter. Instead, a single local block collects these expressions in a central spot. This fosters a more structured configuration, enabling quick changes. If the naming pattern evolves, editing one local expression updates every resource depending on that name. If the module merges subnets from two lists, switching or adding new subnets in the local expression automates the entire resource setup. This technique is especially valuable when advanced logic or multiple steps are needed.

Let us take an example wherein there is a module that deploys a virtual machine, with input variables for environment_name and project_prefix:

```
# Locals block inside the module's main.tf
locals {
  vm_name_combined = "${var.project_prefix}-
${var.environment_name}-vm"
  tag_environment  = upper(var.environment_name)
}
resource "azurerm_linux_virtual_machine" "primary_vm" {
  name                = local.vm_name_combined
  resource_group_name = var.resource_group_name
  location            = var.location
  # A separate map of tags referencing a local
  tags = {
    Environment = local.tag_environment
    Project     = var.project_prefix
  }
  # additional config...
}
```

Here, vm_name_combined merges the prefix and environment into one cohesive resource name, while tag_environment converts environment_name to uppercase for consistent tagging. If the naming convention or environment changes, the local references ensure that every block updates automatically, preventing resource sprawl or code duplication. Also, limiting logic to a local expression ensures that future contributors can easily identify how naming conventions or merges happen, rather than chasing logic across multiple resource blocks. Locals further maintain the boundary between what end users control and the module's internal details, clarifying the difference between user-supplied variables and derived computed values.

# Module Outputs

We very often rely on module outputs to expose crucial data once the module finishes creating or configuring resources. This data might be as simple as an identifier (for instance, a VNet ID in Azure or an instance ID in AWS) or as complex as a list of DNS names or machine IP addresses. These outputs serve a central role by letting other parts of the configuration reference values without tightly coupling to resource internals. A single module could create multiple resources, store them in a private subnet, and produce only a few relevant details needed by the rest of the infrastructure. By doing so, the module maintains a tidy boundary and ensures that consumers, such as other modules or parent configurations, do not have to sift through or replicate all the logic in the child module. This arrangement also helps evolve the module over time. If new attributes become critical (like database endpoints or advanced tags), developers can include new outputs without breaking existing consumers that rely on older outputs. Here, one compelling practice is to add a concise description that clarifies why a particular output is included or how it should be interpreted, improving code clarity for future team members.

A specific example is a module that creates an Azure virtual machine. Suppose the module might output the resource ID, the assigned public IP address, and a series of tags. In the module's outputs.tf file, code might read:

```
output "vm_id" {
  description = "Unique ID of the Azure virtual machine"
  value       = azurerm_linux_virtual_machine.main.id
}
output "vm_public_ip" {
  description = "Public IP address of the virtual machine"
  value       = azurerm_public_ip.main.ip_address
}
```

Upon running terraform apply, the root configuration can retrieve these values as module.vm_module.vm_id or module.vm_module.vm_public_ip. If a subsequent part of the infrastructure needs to store or reference that IP, it can do so without rewriting or duplicating the module's internal details. This separation proves especially useful when multiple modules must coordinate. For instance, a networking module might need to attach a security rule referencing the VM's IP, or a monitoring module might log the IP for external checks.

## Write My First Module

The easiest way to experience the advantages of modules is to create one from start to finish. A frequently cited example involves managing an Azure resource group and a virtual network together, making them easily replicable in different environments.

So here, let us begin by creating a folder named azure_vnet_module, containing three main files: **variables.tf**, **main.tf**, and outputs.tf. In **variables.tf**, we list the parameters that users can provide, for instance resource_group_name, location, vnet_name, and address_space as below:

```
variable "resource_group_name" {
  type        = string
  description = "Name of the resource group"
}
variable "location" {
  type        = string
  description = "Azure region for all resources"
}
variable "vnet_name" {
  type        = string
  description = "Name of the virtual network"
  default     = "default-vnet"
}
variable "address_space" {
  type        = list(string)
  description = "Address space for the VNet"
  default     = ["10.0.0.0/16"]
}
```

The module's **main.tf** references these variables to build resources. One block may define the resource group, and another block may define the virtual network:

```
resource "azurerm_resource_group" "demo_rg" {
  name     = var.resource_group_name
  location = var.location
}
resource "azurerm_virtual_network" "demo_vnet" {
  name                = var.vnet_name
  resource_group_name = azurerm_resource_group.demo_rg.name
  location            = var.location
  address_space       = var.address_space
}
```

Finally, in outputs.tf, expose essential details for downstream usage:

```
output "vnet_id" {
  description = "ID of the virtual network"
  value       = azurerm_virtual_network.demo_vnet.id
}
```

Once this module is available in azure_vnet_module, the root configuration can call it:

```
module "my_network" {
  source              = "./azure_vnet_module"
  resource_group_name = "rg-shared"
  location            = "EastUS"
  vnet_name           = "vnet-staging"
}
```

That minimal snippet constructs a reusable pattern for building resource groups and virtual networks. If additional environments require a similar architecture, the same module can be invoked with different variable assignments. Each environment remains consistent in naming, structure, and best practices, easing tasks such as cost control and troubleshooting. One might add submodules for creating subnets or security rules, or provide extra variables for fine-tuning properties.

# Nested Modules

Many teams prefer to break large components into smaller modules, each handling a distinct part of the infrastructure. One example is a network module that sets up a virtual network (VNet) and a nested module that configures subnets within that network. Suppose there is a parent module named azure_network, which expects inputs such as resource_group_name, location, and vnet_name. It creates the virtual network in its **`main.tf`**. Within that same folder, the parent module can call a child module named azure_subnet to define subnets for the newly created VNet. The child module might live in a subdirectory called modules/azure_subnet and contain logic for a single subnet, including the name, address_prefix, and reference to the parent's vnet_name.

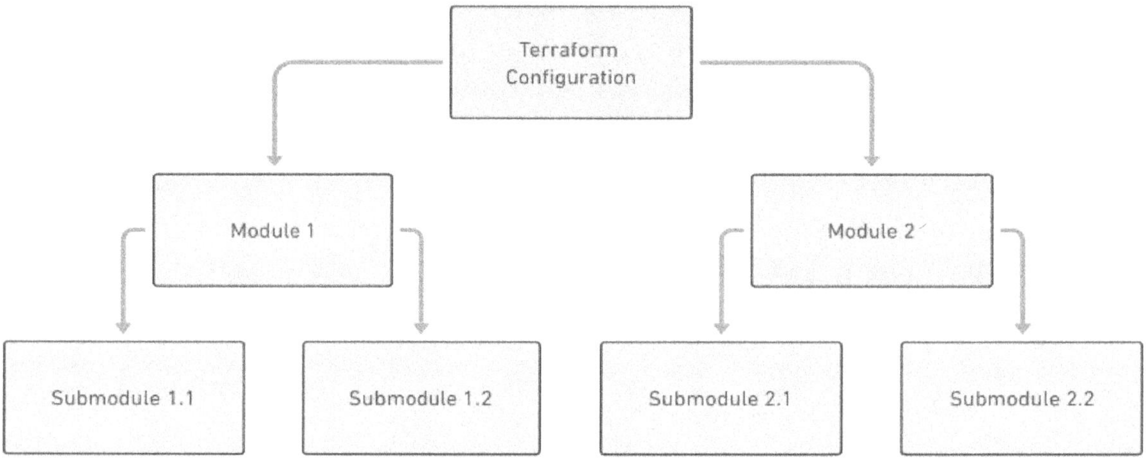


**Fig 4.2 Nested Modules**

Let us think of a scenario where the parent module's **`main.tf`** references the child module. First, it defines the VNet:

```
resource "azurerm_virtual_network" "parent_vnet" {
  name                = var.vnet_name
  resource_group_name = var.resource_group_name
  location            = var.location
  address_space       = ["10.0.0.0/16"]
}
```

Then, it calls a child module:

```
module "subnet_module" {
```

```
  source                      = "./modules/azure_subnet"
  resource_group_name         = var.resource_group_name
  vnet_name                   =
azurerm_virtual_network.parent_vnet.name
  subnet_name                 = var.subnet_name
  subnet_address_prefix       = var.subnet_address_prefix
}
```

Inside modules/azure_subnet, code references the inputs for creating a subnet:

```
variable "resource_group_name" { type = string }
variable "vnet_name" { type = string }
variable "subnet_name" { type = string }
variable "subnet_address_prefix" { type = string }
resource "azurerm_subnet" "child_subnet" {
  name                   = var.subnet_name
  resource_group_name    = var.resource_group_name
  virtual_network_name = var.vnet_name
  address_prefixes       = [var.subnet_address_prefix]
}
```

This pattern helps combine multiple modules without mixing all resources in one file. The parent module focuses on high-level structure (like the VNet plus subnets), while each child submodule handles a narrower set of resources. You can then expand or replace submodules independently, passing new variables down the chain. This style scales to more sophisticated designs: a main infrastructure module might call submodules for compute, storage, and security, each with its own logic and data definitions.

# Implement Module Versioning

The versioning feature makes sure that changes to a module won't break existing environments by accident. A common approach is to store module code in a Git repository, tag each release, and reference that release in the Terraform configuration. This process involves creating or updating a module on GitHub, then tagging a commit to represent a stable release, such as v1.x.

Following is an overview of the steps involved:

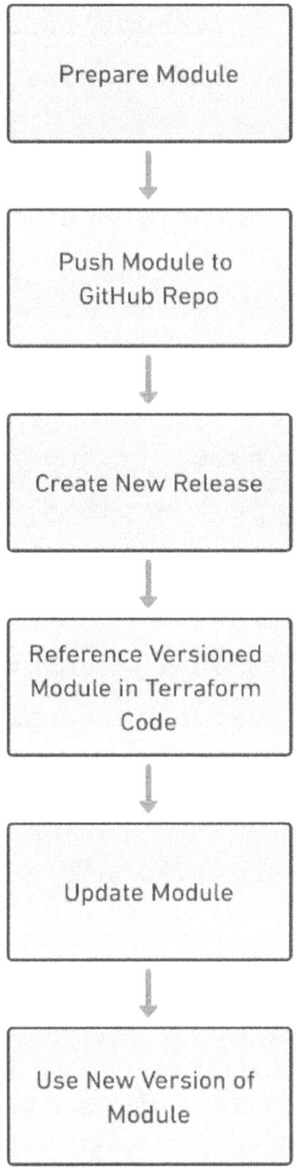


**Fig 4.3 Steps to Implement Model Versioning**

Suppose the code is in *https://github.com/example-org/terraform-azure-vnet*. The repository might store an azure_vnet module that sets up a virtual network. Whenever you are ready to publish a stable iteration, you create a release in GitHub with a semantic version tag like v1.2.1. Within your Terraform configuration, you reference that exact version:

```
module "prod_vnet" {
```

```
  source  = "git::https://github.com/example-org/terraform-azure-vnet.git//azure_vnet?ref=v1.2.1"
  resource_group_name = "rg-production"
  location            = "EastUS"
  vnet_name           = "prod-vnet"
}
```

In the above, it instructs Terraform to download the module code from the azure_vnet folder at that v1.2.1 Git tag, thus freezing the module's code to a stable version. If a developer later modifies the module for new features or bug fixes, they can push changes and create a new tag, for instance v1.2.2. Consumers can decide whether to upgrade by adjusting their ref. This approach avoids pulling in untested code inadvertently and allows each environment to choose when to adopt new versions. Some organizations add a version block in a Terraform Registry or package the modules in a private registry. The principle remains: each environment pins a module version, achieving reproducible builds. If module functionality grows significantly, maintainers might release v2.0.0 to flag potential compatibility breaks.

# Summary

Overall, the idea of Terraform modules was one of the most important topics covered in this chapter. We investigated the manner in which modules, at their fundamental level, enclose a collection of infrastructure resources that can be used together. We gained an understanding of the operation of modules by focusing on its three fundamental components: inputs, locals, and outputs. We learned the practical application of nested modules as a means of further modularizing infrastructure components after gaining an understanding of how to define, reference, and apply modules. The configuration will be much simpler to comprehend and administer if you use nested modules since they produce a hierarchical structure that is analogous to the structure of the system you are developing.

And finally, we learned how to implement version control by observing how modules are managed when they are hosted on services like GitHub. We also learned to upgrade a module and switch to a new version without causing any disruption to the deployments that are already in place.

# CHAPTER 5: TERRAFORM STATE MANAGEMENT

# Understanding Terraform State

Terraform uses a state file to keep track of the real-world resources under its management. Whenever you run commands like **`terraform plan`** or **`terraform apply`**, Terraform consults the state file to figure out which resources already exist, how they're configured, and what changes are needed. This file is typically named **`terraform.tfstate`** in a local setup, and it gets updated after each successful apply. A simple scenario is when you create an Azure Resource Group. Terraform records its name, ID, and other metadata in the state. If you later update the location or add a new tag, Terraform compares your latest configuration against the stored data to see what changed. This mechanism saves time because Terraform does not have to query the entire infrastructure every time; it instead references the snapshot in the state file and identifies the delta between the declared configuration and current reality. However, the state file can contain sensitive details like credentials or keys if your resources require them, so it demands secure handling. Team members also benefit from having a single authoritative version of the state, ensuring everyone's environment stays consistent.

Although the state file is central to Terraform's workflows, many realize it can be manually manipulated if unusual or emergency tasks arise. For example, if a resource was deleted outside of Terraform—perhaps in the Azure portal—one can remove it from Terraform's perspective with **`terraform state rm`**. Another subcommand, **`terraform state mv`**, renames or moves resources between modules in the state, avoiding an unintended destruction-and-recreation cycle. These direct manipulations carry risk: an incorrect move or removal can cause Terraform to lose track of live resources. You must carefully weigh whether the benefits of manual changes outweigh the potential for mistakes. In addition, the **`terraform refresh`** command synchronizes resource attributes with the current infrastructure, updating the state with real-time information from your provider. This procedure is especially useful if external processes modify the infrastructure, causing discrepancies. While the state file is powerful for normal operations, the best approach is to rely on standard code modifications and **`terraform apply`** for routine tasks, using direct state manipulation only when truly necessary.

# Local vs Remote State

Individuals working solo or on small-scale experiments often keep the state file locally, which is convenient for rapid iteration. In this local configuration, a file named **`terraform.tfstate`** appears in the project folder after initialization and changes with each apply. No extra setup is required, so it suits quick proofs-of-concept or personal sandbox environments. However, storing the state file locally makes collaboration and security more complicated. If multiple developers share a code repository, each might manage a different local state, risking conflicts if they run Terraform at the same time. Additionally, the local file could contain secrets or resource attributes that you may not want on every developer's machine. If the local disk fails or is not backed up, recovering from a lost state file can be messy, leading to possible resource duplication or confusion about how to handle existing deployments.

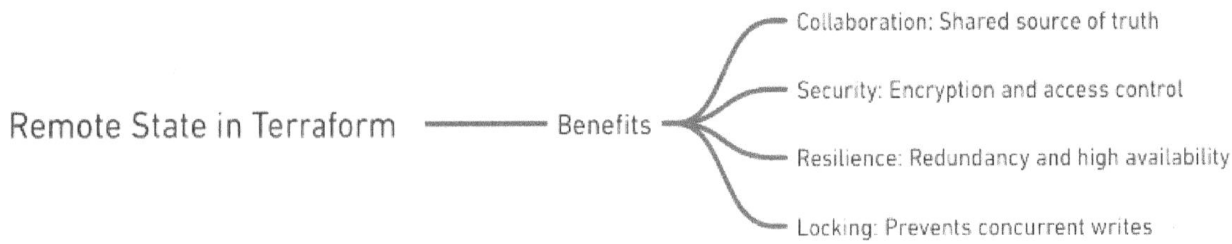


**Fig 5.1 Remote State in Terraform**

Teams typically adopt remote state to avoid these drawbacks. By storing the Terraform state in a shared location, such as AWS S3, Azure Blob Storage, Google Cloud Storage, or Terraform Cloud, everyone uses a single, authoritative reference. The main configuration includes a **`backend`** block specifying credentials and endpoints for the remote state. Upon running **`terraform init`**, Terraform migrates the local state to the remote backend (assuming you confirm when prompted). Now, every plan or apply reads from and writes to that shared location, ensuring that no developer inadvertently diverges from the official infrastructure record. Remote backends often support locking, preventing multiple users from updating the state at the same time. They can also include server-side encryption, versioning, or replication, enhancing security and durability.

Following is a quick example for Azure:

```
terraform {
  backend "azurerm" {
    resource_group_name  = "myStateRG"
    storage_account_name = "mystatestore"
    container_name       = "tfstate"
    key                  = "global.tfstate"
  }
}
```

The above one ensures that all updates go directly into an Azure container.

# Implementing Remote State in Terraform Configuration

It is very oftenly observed that teams in team-based environments often shift to remote state for higher collaboration and security. Instead of storing a local **terraform.tfstate** file, each plan or apply reads from a shared backend. This approach removes the risk of conflicting local copies or lost state data and ensures that every contributor references an authoritative source. A typical setup might involve Azure Blob Storage, AWS S3, or Terraform Cloud. The remote storage can handle encryption, versioning, and locking. This leads to consistent infrastructure changes, even when multiple individuals run Terraform simultaneously.

Following is an example that involves editing a configuration to include a backend block, then reinitializing.

```
terraform {
  backend "azurerm" {
    resource_group_name  = "rg-tfstate"
    storage_account_name = "mystatestorage"
    container_name       = "tfstate"
    key                  = "myproj.tfstate"
  }
}
```

When you run terraform init, it'll migrate any existing local state to the remote backend, as long as you confirm. After that, commands will update the remote file, making sure everything's in sync.

# State Manipulation

Terraform occasionally requires manual adjustments to the state file, though best practices encourage minimal direct changes. Scenarios like moving a resource between modules or cleaning up entries for a resource manually deleted in a cloud console prompt the use of **terraform state** subcommands. If a resource has been removed outside of Terraform, you can run terraform state rm to remove it from the file and avoid unwanted re-creation.

For example:

```
terraform state rm azurerm_virtual_machine.example
```

Another subcommand, terraform state mv, renames or relocates resources within the file. If code is refactored, one can preserve the existing resource without destruction and recreation by running something like:

```
terraform state mv azurerm_virtual_machine.example
module.new_struct.azurerm_virtual_machine.example
```

These operations need to be reviewed carefully because if you make a mistake, it can mess up the infrastructure's current state and the state that Terraform recorded. It's a good idea to back up the file and then confirm any changes with a Terraform plan.

# State Conflicts

State conflicts in Terraform typically arise in situations where multiple team members are working on the same infrastructure simultaneously, or when there are manual changes to the infrastructure outside of Terraform. These situations lead to inconsistencies between the actual infrastructure and the Terraform state file, causing conflicts when Terraform attempts to apply changes.

Let us proceed to explore some common situations of conflicts and how to resolve them:

## Concurrent Terraform Operations

When multiple team members execute Terraform commands concurrently, they might encounter state lock errors. Terraform uses state locking to prevent others from running Terraform commands that could conflict. However, in some scenarios, the lock might not be released, leading to a conflict.

To resolve this, you can manually unlock the state file using the terraform force-unlock command. However, it's essential to be sure that the previous Terraform operation is indeed not running as forcing the unlock can cause state corruption.

```
terraform force-unlock LOCK_ID
```

## Drift Management

Drift happens when the actual infrastructure setup diverges from the state stored in the Terraform state file. This can occur when changes are made to the infrastructure outside of Terraform, such as manual modifications or automated processes.

To manage and correct drift, you can use the terraform refresh command to update the state file with the actual infrastructure state. After the state file is updated, **`terraform plan`** can show the difference between the current state and the desired state. If the drift is acceptable, the state file can be left as is. If not, you can use **`terraform apply`** to reconcile the differences.

## Manual Changes to State File

If you've manually edited the state file and inadvertently introduced conflicts or errors, the

**`terraform validate`** command can be used to check the syntax of the Terraform files, and **`terraform plan`** can be used to check the state file's validity.

In case of an error, you can restore the state from a backup if available. If not, you might need to manually fix the state file or use the terraform state rm command to remove the problematic resources and import them back using terraform import.

## Inconsistent Resource Metadata

Sometimes, Terraform may fail to apply changes due to inconsistencies between resource metadata in the state file and the actual configuration files. This can occur when moving or renaming resources or modules without using the appropriate commands.

In such situations, you can use the terraform state mv command to correctly rename or move the resources in the state file. This command updates the state file to reflect the new location or name of the resource, resolving the conflict.

# State Drift and Reconciliation

In the realm of Terraform, the term "drift" is used to denote any divergence between the actual state of the infrastructure and the state recorded in the Terraform state file. The phenomenon of drift may occur due to multiple reasons such as manual changes to the infrastructure outside of Terraform, automatic updates made by cloud providers, or even inadvertent modifications due to software bugs.

Drift management is a critical part of maintaining IaC, as the undetected or unmanaged drift can lead to unpredictable Terraform behavior, unforeseen dependencies, or discrepancies in reporting. It is also essential for compliance and governance, as infrastructure drift might lead to potential vulnerabilities and security breaches.

Following is a step-by-step overview of how drift can occur:

- **Initiation**: We use Terraform to create or update infrastructure. Once the **`terraform apply`** command is executed, Terraform stores the current state of the infrastructure in the state file.
- **Drift Occurrence**: Changes are made to the infrastructure outside of Terraform. This could be manual changes, such as someone modifying a virtual machine's settings in the Azure portal, or automated changes, such as an auto-scaling policy increasing the number of instances.
- **Detection**: The next time you run **`terraform plan`** or terraform apply, Terraform compares the desired state (as defined by the Terraform configuration) with the current state (as defined by the state file) and the actual state (the real infrastructure). In this process, Terraform detects the drift – any difference between the actual state and the current state.

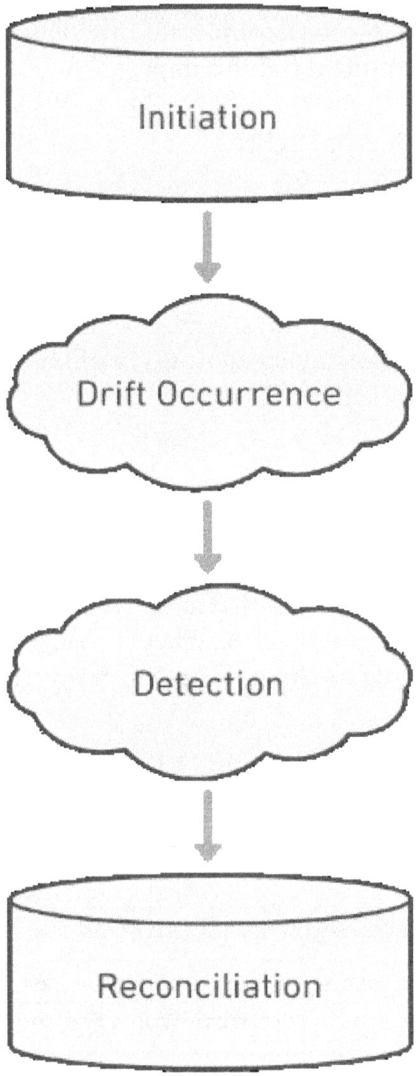


**Fig 5.2 Drift Occurence Process**

- **Reconciliation**: Reconciliation of the drift in Terraform can be achieved by using the terraform refresh command followed by terraform apply. The refresh command updates the state file with the actual state of the infrastructure, allowing you to see the drift when you run terraform plan.

```
# Update the state file with the real infrastructure
```

```
terraform refresh

# Check the differences between the desired, current and actual state

terraform plan
```

Once you've assessed the changes presented by the plan command, you can decide whether to:

- **Reconcile the Drift Automatically**: If the drift is acceptable or expected (e.g., an auto-scaling event), you might just want to update the state file to match the actual infrastructure. Here, you simply run the **`terraform apply`** to align the state file with the desired state and actual infrastructure state.
- **Undo the Drift Manually**: If the drift was due to an unauthorized or undesirable change, you might need to manually revert the change in the infrastructure and then run terraform refresh to update the state file.

# State Migration

State migration in Terraform refers to the process of moving resources within or between Terraform states. The need for state migration arises under several circumstances, including but not limited to:

- **Refactoring Terraform Configurations**: As the infrastructure grows and changes, you might need to reorganize the Terraform configurations for better manageability or modularity. Such refactoring may involve moving resources from one configuration (or module) to another, which requires state migration to avoid destroying and recreating the same resources.
- **Adopting Remote State Storage**: If you initially use local state storage and later decide to switch to remote state storage for collaboration or security reasons, you need to migrate the state from the local backend to the remote backend.
- **Switching Between Remote Backends**: For instance, you may want to switch from an Azure Blob Storage backend to a Terraform Cloud backend due to organization policy changes or service upgrades. This also involves state migration.

The terraform state mv command is the key to state migration in Terraform. This command allows you to move resources within a state or between states, effectively changing the resource address recorded in the state.

Let us look at an example of migrating an Azure virtual machine from a module (module.old) to the root module:

```
terraform state mv module.old.azurerm_virtual_machine.example
azurerm_virtual_machine.example
```

This command tells Terraform to change the address of the specified resource in the state, avoiding the need to destroy and recreate the resource in the process. Please note that you should revise the Terraform configurations to reflect the address change before running **terraform apply** again.

When it comes to migrating state between backends, you first need to initialize the new backend with **terraform init** and specify the new backend configuration. When prompted by Terraform, agree to copy the state to the new backend:

```
terraform init -backend-config="new-backend.hcl"

# Terraform will ask for the confirmation to copy state to the
new backend

Do you want to copy existing state to the new backend?

  Pre-existing state was found while migrating the previous
"local" backend to the

  newly configured "azurerm" backend. No existing state was
found in the newly

  configured "azurerm" backend. Do you want to copy this state
to the new "azurerm"

  backend? Enter "yes" to copy and "no" to start with an empty
state.

  Enter a value: yes
```

As a best practice, always back up the state before performing state migrations and test the process in a non-production environment if possible.

# Summary

So, in this chapter, we took a look at the whole idea of Terraform state, which is a key part of how Terraform manages and tracks infrastructure. We found out that the state file basically keeps a record of the resources that Terraform has created, which lets it keep the infrastructure and configuration in sync. We also checked out local and remote states, comparing the two to better understand how they work and when to use them.

Then, we moved on to state manipulation, learning how to do it and what it means. We used practical examples to understand how to use the terraform state mv command to move and rename resources, which lets us refactor our Terraform configurations without affecting the actual infrastructure. We also explored potential state conflicts and learned to resolve them using the state command. Lastly, we delved into state drift, reconciliation, and migration. We learned how changes in infrastructure outside of Terraform can cause drift from the state file. We learned that by running the terraform refresh command, we can update the state file to match the real infrastructure, essentially reconciling state drift.

# CHAPTER 6: PROVISIONERS AND PROVISIONING RESOURCES

# Introduction to Infrastructure Provisioning

Infrastructure provisioning is the process of transforming a design for servers, networks, and services into tangible, running resources. In the past, administrators tackled this by manually creating and configuring machines, databases, and load balancers. Over time, teams realized manual steps could lead to errors, inconsistent environments, and slow turnaround. Modern practices like IaC address these challenges. By defining an environment using code – for example, specifying a virtual network, subnet, and virtual machine in a file – tools such as Terraform can automatically create the specified resources in a repeatable manner.

For instance, consider setting up a multi-tier web application. Without IaC, an administrator might sign into a cloud console, click through wizards for each piece (network, VM, database), and manually link them together. If a second environment is needed for testing, they must replicate these steps – prone to missing a detail or forgetting a configuration. Automated provisioning replaces these steps with code that references the relevant resource parameters. A developer can clone or reuse that code, change environment-specific variables, then let Terraform create an identical environment. This consistency eliminates drift between dev and prod and streamlines bug resolution, because all environments share the same baseline configuration.

The benefits of codified provisioning extend beyond consistency. Version control systems (e.g., Git) store each infrastructure definition, providing an audit trail of changes. When an environment breaks after a commit, you can revert to a previous known-good version. Infrastructure provisioning code can also incorporate best practices for security and performance, ensuring new deployments inherit recommended configurations. Additionally, ephemeral or short-lived environments become practical, because spinning up or down entire sets of resources is as simple as running a Terraform command. This ephemeral approach helps optimize cost and fosters frequent testing. The following sections explore how Terraform implements provisioning logic through "provisioners," bridging resource creation and post-creation setup tasks.

Although Terraform can manage everything from networking and storage to load balancers, certain tasks – like installing packages on a newly launched VM – do not always have direct resource equivalents. Provisioners help fill these gaps by allowing final scripting or file transfers after a resource is created. For example, you might upload a shell script via Terraform, then run it to configure security patches. Provisioners operate outside Terraform's primary model, so you should use them only when no better option exists. If the cloud provider's native resource or a dedicated configuration management tool (like Ansible) can handle the same actions, that path usually yields a more stable, maintainable solution.

# Built-In Provisioners

Terraform offers four main built-in provisioners: **`file`**, **`local-exec`**, **`remote-exec`**, and **`null_resource`**. Each addresses slightly different scenarios. The file provisioner copies local files to a remote machine, letting you transfer scripts, config files, or entire directories. The local-exec provisioner executes a command on the same machine running Terraform, suitable for tasks like calling external APIs or updating a local database of resource IDs. The remote-exec provisioner logs into the newly created resource (commonly via SSH or WinRM) to run commands – a popular choice for installing software on a VM. Lastly, null_resource is a special "dummy" resource that can house provisioners without associating them to a real infrastructure resource.

Each provisioner triggers either on resource creation or removal, depending on your configuration. If a provisioner fails, Terraform typically marks the resource as "tainted." On the next run, Terraform tears it down and tries again. This can be disruptive for production systems if minor provisioning issues cause the entire resource to get rebuilt. Additionally, these scripts do not automatically re-run on resource updates. If you require ongoing changes, a dedicated config-management tool is usually more robust. Still, for tasks that must occur at creation time – like uploading custom SSL certificates or running a short initialization script – Terraform's provisioners do the job effectively when used carefully.

## File Provisioner

The file provisioner copies files or directories from your local system to the resource upon creation. As a quick demonstration, imagine you have an Azure Linux VM and want to upload a shell script to /home/azureuser.

So here, you start by defining your VM with an accessible SSH public IP:

```
resource "azurerm_linux_virtual_machine" "demo_vm" {
  name                = "demoVM"
  location            = azurerm_resource_group.rg.location
  resource_group_name = azurerm_resource_group.rg.name
  size                = "Standard_B1s"
  admin_username = "azureuser"
  disable_password_authentication = true
  network_interface_ids =
[azurerm_network_interface.demo_nic.id]
  os_disk {
    caching              = "ReadWrite"
    storage_account_type = "Standard_LRS"
  }
  source_image_reference {
```

```
    publisher = "Canonical"
    offer     = "UbuntuServer"
    sku       = "18.04-LTS"
    version   = "latest"
  }
  # Key-based SSH authentication
  admin_ssh_key {
    username   = "azureuser"
    public_key = file("~/.ssh/id_rsa.pub")
  }
  # Additional config...
}
```

Next, attach a file provisioner:

```
provisioner "file" {
  source      = "setup.sh"
  destination = "/home/azureuser/setup.sh"
  connection {
    type        = "ssh"
    user        = "azureuser"
    private_key = file("~/.ssh/id_rsa")
    host        = azurerm_public_ip.demo_vm_ip.ip_address
  }
}
```

Here, **setup.sh** is a local file that might install packages or set environment variables. By the time Terraform finishes creating the VM, it runs the file provisioner, uploading the script to the remote path. The connection block uses the same SSH key specified in the VM resource. If the script is large or you want to transfer an entire directory, set **source = "my_folder"** and **destination = "/home/azureuser/my_folder"**. Once uploading completes, you might follow up with a remote-exec step to run setup.sh. This approach eliminates the need to manually scp files. However, watch for timing issues: if SSH is not fully ready or the IP hasn't fully propagated, the file upload might fail.

## Local-Exec Provisioner

The local-exec provisioner runs a command or script on your local machine after a resource is created. Suppose you create a storage account in Azure, and once the account exists, you want to run a local shell script that populates it with some initial data as below:

```
resource "azurerm_storage_account" "my_storage" {
  name                     = "mystoraccount"
  resource_group_name      = azurerm_resource_group.rg.name
  location                 =
azurerm_resource_group.rg.location
  account_tier             = "Standard"
  account_replication_type = "LRS"
  provisioner "local-exec" {
    command = "./populate_storage.sh
${self.primary_access_key}"
  }
}
```

In this scenario, Terraform finishes creating the storage account, then triggers local-exec. The **command** references a local script, **populate_storage.sh**, and passes the storage account's primary access key as an argument. The script presumably uses Azure CLI or a REST call to add initial files or data. Keep in mind that local-exec runs on the same workstation or CI server executing terraform apply. If that local environment lacks Azure CLI or is missing environment variables, the script may fail. As a result, local-exec can introduce machine-specific dependencies and hamper reproducibility unless carefully documented or placed in a consistent build environment.

Another usage of local-exec is sending notifications or logging. For instance, you might do:

```
provisioner "local-exec" {
  command = <<EOT
curl -X POST -H "Content-Type: application/json" \
  -d '{"text": "New storage account created:
${azurerm_storage_account.my_storage.name}"}' \
```

```
  https://hooks.slack.com/services/XXXXXXX
EOT
}
```

This means every time the storage account is freshly created, a Slack message is posted. If you refactor your code to rename the resource, or if the creation fails mid-way, you might see partial messages. As with other provisioners, treat local-exec as a last resort for tasks not better handled by the cloud itself or a dedicated pipeline.

## Remote-Exec Provisioner

Now, when you want to run commands inside the new resource, remote-exec is your friend. For example, you spin up an Ubuntu VM in Azure and need to install Nginx. After the resource is created, remote-exec connects via SSH and executes:

```
resource "azurerm_linux_virtual_machine" "web_vm" {
  # (the usual VM config)
  provisioner "remote-exec" {
    inline = [
      "sudo apt-get update",
      "sudo apt-get install -y nginx",
      "sudo systemctl start nginx"
    ]
    connection {
      type        = "ssh"
      user        = "azureuser"
      private_key = file("~/.ssh/id_rsa")
      host        = azurerm_public_ip.web_vm_ip.ip address
    }
  }
}
```

Once Terraform sees the VM is up, it attempts to SSH with the specified user and key. If successful, it runs apt-get update, installs Nginx, and starts the service. This method is convenient for small initializations, yet it is generally not recommended for significant or ongoing configuration tasks. If the command set is large, you might store them in a shell script, and use

```
inline = ["bash /home/azureuser/configure.sh"]
```

Another tactic is combining remote-exec with the file provisioner. First upload your script with file, then execute it with remote-exec. If anything fails, Terraform marks the VM as tainted, which on the next run leads to a destroy/recreate cycle. If partial installs are common, or if re-running a script is harmful, you must carefully design the commands to be idempotent or resilient to multiple attempts.

An interesting advantage of remote-exec is that you can dynamically retrieve resource attributes. For example, if a certain environment variable or IP address is only known after creation, you could read them in the script. However, the code becomes more ephemeral, living only in your shell commands or external files, which can hamper clarity. Another detail is connection readiness. New VMs may take 30–60 seconds to fully boot and open SSH. Terraform tries connecting almost immediately. If that fails, it either retries for a short while or eventually times out.

## Null Resource and Additional Patterns

The null_resource is a unique construct for tasks that do not map to a specific resource. Suppose you want to run a provisioning step purely based on changes to certain variables or references. You define a null_resource with triggers referencing those items, causing the provisioner to re-run whenever the triggers change.

For instance, if you want to run a local script every time your app version changes:

```
resource "null_resource" "notify_deploy" {
  triggers = {
    app_version = var.app_version
  }
  provisioner "local-exec" {
    command = "echo Deploying version ${var.app_version}..."
  }
}
```

Here, whenever the app_version variable updates, Terraform sees the triggers key differ, taints the null_resource, and re-runs the local-exec. Another usage might be after building a Docker image, you push a notification. However, sprinkling too many null_resources can create a procedural mess within an otherwise declarative codebase.

There are some advanced patterns revolve around using the file provisioner plus remote-exec to install configuration managers like Chef or Ansible on a newly minted VM, letting them handle the rest of the OS configuration. Alternatively, you can parse outputs from remote-exec commands for advanced logic, though that gets precarious. Because provisioners exist outside Terraform's standard model, you do not get the same idempotent or dependency-based logic that normal resources enjoy. If your environment demands frequent updates or reconfiguration, consider a specialized approach. Use Terraform for resource definitions, then rely on a config management solution or CI pipeline for ongoing changes. This separation keeps your Terraform code simpler and less fragile.

All said, the built-in provisioners in Terraform can be extremely helpful for bridging final setup tasks, especially for small or one-off actions. Here, you avoid tying large, complex system changes to a single remote-exec step. Instead, let Terraform handle resource creation and use a dedicated method (like cloud-init or user-data on AWS, or Azure custom data) for more robust instance configuration.

# Using Provisioners for Configuration Management

Provisioners in Terraform allow you to run scripts or commands on newly created resources, effectively bridging the gap between simple resource creation and more extensive configuration management tasks. While Terraform excels at provisioning cloud infrastructure (like networks, storage, or VMs), it does not natively orchestrate deeper OS-level or application-level settings. That is typically the domain of tools like Ansible, Chef, or Puppet. Nonetheless, provisioners can provide a practical stopgap in cases where the user needs immediate or small-scale configuration changes without adopting a full-fledged configuration management framework. The simplest scenario might be installing a single package or uploading an SSL certificate, all triggered automatically once a VM is instantiated.

To illustrate a typical approach, suppose your environment includes a load balancer, multiple Linux web servers, and a shared database. Terraform's primary job is spinning up the LB, servers, and DB in your chosen cloud. However, once a server is running, you might want to install Nginx, place a new index.html, and set up a systemd service. One path is to rely on Terraform's remote-exec provisioner to run apt-get install -y nginx. Another path is to copy a script that performs these tasks (using the file provisioner) and then invoke it. We will look into a more in-depth example combining the two:

```
resource "azurerm_linux_virtual_machine" "web_vm" {
  name                = "webvm1"
  location            = azurerm_resource_group.rg.location
  resource_group_name = azurerm_resource_group.rg.name
```

```
  size                   = "Standard_B1s"
  admin_username = "ubuntu"
  disable_password_authentication = true
  network_interface_ids =
[azurerm_network_interface.web_nic.id]
  os_disk {
    storage_account_type = "Standard_LRS"
  }
  source_image_reference {
    publisher = "Canonical"
    offer     = "UbuntuServer"
    sku       = "20_04-lts"
    version   = "latest"
  }
  admin_ssh_key {
    username   = "ubuntu"
    public_key = file("~/.ssh/id_rsa.pub")
  }
  # 1) Use file provisioner to copy our custom config script
  provisioner "file" {
    source      = "configure_web.sh"
    destination = "/home/ubuntu/configure_web.sh"
    connection {
      type        = "ssh"
      user        = "ubuntu"
      private_key = file("~/.ssh/id_rsa")
      host        = azurerm_public_ip.web_vm_ip.ip_address
    }
  }
```

```
  # 2) Use remote-exec to run that script
  provisioner "remote-exec" {
    inline = [
      "chmod +x /home/ubuntu/configure_web.sh",
      "/home/ubuntu/configure_web.sh"
    ]
    connection {
      type        = "ssh"
      user        = "ubuntu"
      private_key = file("~/.ssh/id_rsa")
      host        = azurerm_public_ip.web_vm_ip.ip_address
    }
  }
}
```

In the above sample program, **configure_web.sh** might handle installing Nginx, copying index files from a repo, and adjusting firewall settings for an HTTP-based service. However, it also has drawbacks: if your environment changes after creation—for example, you want to add a new site or rotate a certificate—the original provisioner does not re-run automatically. You might rely on re-creating the VM or manually applying changes. This is why experts caution that large-scale or ongoing configuration is better handled by a tool specialized in that domain. But if the changes are modest, ephemeral, or only relevant at creation time, a well-crafted script plus provisioners can suffice.

Another angle is to "bootstrap" a real configuration management tool. For instance, you might run remote-exec to install the Ansible agent or Chef client on the new server, then let that agent handle the rest. The advantage is that you avoid building a huge set of inline provisioning commands in Terraform. Instead, you use a single step:

```
provisioner "remote-exec" {
  inline = [
    "curl https://example.com/install_ansible_agent.sh -o
/tmp/install_ansible.sh",
    "chmod +x /tmp/install_ansible.sh",
    "/tmp/install_ansible.sh"
```

```
  ]
}
```

That script can register the server with an Ansible control node or Chef server, from which point the environment is managed outside Terraform. This pattern merges Terraform's strength in resource orchestration with mature config management solutions that keep VMs consistent over time.

There are also times when local-exec helps in config management. Imagine you want to handle firewall rules with an external script that talks to your on-premise firewall. After each new VM is created, you might run a local script that registers the new IP in your firewall's rules. That script runs on the same machine as Terraform, using local environment variables for authentication. This is config management in the sense that you are orchestrating an outside service's configuration (the firewall). Still, you must weigh the risk of tying external tasks to your local environment.

# Summary

To conclude, we dove further into our understanding of Terraform provisioners to get the full picture. After gaining a concept of resource provisioning as a starting point, we discovered how it plays an essential role in the deployment of infrastructure by assisting in the configuration and startup of servers, apps, and other components.

We took a more in-depth look at the many sorts of in-built provisioners that are available through Terraform, examining the specific use cases for each one as well as the steps to build it. This included the local-exec provisioner, which enables executing scripts locally on the system running Terraform, as well as the remote-exec provisioner, which enables running commands on the resource that is being created or changed. Additionally, this included the file provisioner, which copies files or directories to a destination location. We also went over the null resource provisioner, which is a one-of-a-kind piece of software that correlates provisioning activities with any arbitrary collection of adjustments. In addition, we investigated the best ways to use provisioners for administration of configuration settings. This included the various faults that can arise throughout the process as well as the methods that can be utilized to properly handle them. In addition to this, it emphasized how essential it is to adhere to industry standards in order to avoid any potential problems.

# Chapter 7: Working with Secrets

# Process Flow of Secrets Management

As we navigate further into our Terraform learning journey, let us focus our attention on a topic that plays a pivotal role in securing any application or service - Secrets. In the context of IT infrastructure and software applications, secrets refer to any form of sensitive data which, if exposed, could lead to unauthorized access and potential data breaches. Secrets could be anything like API keys, database credentials, SSH keys, certificates, tokens, or any other piece of information that provides access to APIs, databases, or other services.

The importance of secrets management cannot be understated. It is a key element of modern infrastructure management and contributes to the overall security posture of an organization. Secrets are like the keys to the kingdom, and therefore, how you manage these keys can determine the safety of the kingdom. Poor management of secrets can lead to a data breach, negatively affecting a company's reputation, causing financial loss, and in some cases, even leading to legal consequences. As we unravel the world of secrets management, it is vital to understand the standard process flow that governs it. This process enables organizations to securely manage sensitive data throughout its lifecycle.

The main steps involved in a typical secrets management process are as follows:

## Secret Generation

All secrets begin with creation. In many organizations, engineers might manually invent random passwords or rely on software to generate robust keys or tokens. Best practices demand these secrets be unique, random, and appropriately sized, significantly reducing the risk of brute-force attacks. This step often includes deciding which kind of secret is needed: Is it a password for a database? An API key for a microservice? Once identified, a secure generation method (e.g., cryptographic libraries) is used. Overly simple or static secrets remain a prime attack vector, so carefully plan complexity and validity intervals.

## Secure Storage

After a secret is generated, store it in a secure vault or similar repository. Never embed secrets in plain text or version control systems like Git. Instead, solutions like Azure Key Vault, HashiCorp Vault, or AWS Secrets Manager handle secrets with cryptographic protections, enabling authorized services or individuals to retrieve them safely. Effective storage extends beyond encryption – it also includes restricted network access, robust authentication, and the principle of least privilege (PoLP). If an unauthorized entity manages to breach storage, encryption plus strict control ensures the data remains inaccessible without keys.

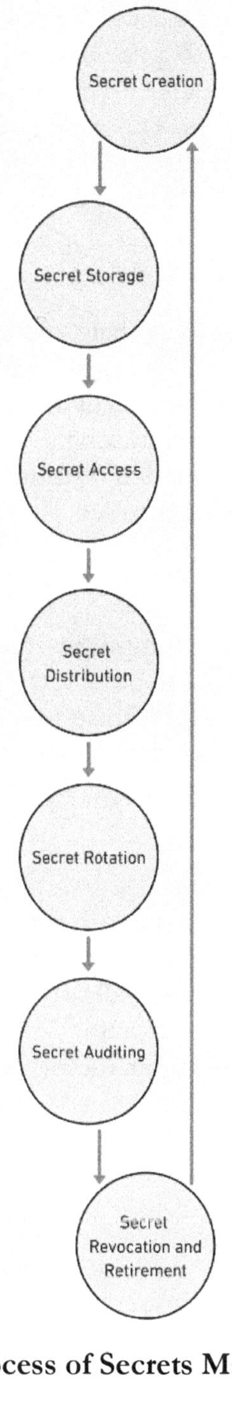


**Fig 7.1 Process of Secrets Management**

## Strict Access Control

A fundamental principle of secrets management is controlling which users or services can see or update which secrets. Implement role-based access or policy-based rules. For instance, an application that requires read-only access to a database password does not need the ability to delete or rotate that password. Proper auditing reveals each request to read or modify secrets, providing visibility into potential anomalies. This gating often relies on identity mechanisms such as Azure AD or tokens from a centralized identity provider. In short, no one obtains a secret unless they are explicitly allowed to do so, reducing accidental or malicious exposure.

## Distribution to Consumers

Secrets must eventually reach services or users that need them, but distribution must be done securely. A service might call the vault's API using an authorized token, retrieving secrets only in memory. Another scenario is injecting secrets as environment variables through a pipeline. This ensures no human handles them directly, minimizing the chance of leaks. Encryption in transit, mutual TLS, or ephemeral tokens further harden distribution. Quick ephemeral retrieval ensures less risk if logs or ephemeral disks are compromised.

## Rotation and Versioning

No secret should last forever. If a secret is compromised, short lifetimes mitigate damage because old secrets quickly become invalid. Regular rotation forces generation of a new secret, invalidating the old one. Tools like Key Vault can store multiple versions of a secret, enabling smooth rollouts. Rotations might be triggered by a time interval or a security event. Proper versioning also helps rollback if a new secret breaks something, or to investigate usage patterns.

## Auditing and Monitoring

Next, secrets management demands continuous surveillance. Monitoring how often secrets are accessed or changed fosters detection of anomalies. If an attacker suddenly tries to read the same secret 100 times, or if a secret is unexpectedly accessed at 3AM, logs can highlight suspicious activity. Azure Key Vault integrates with Azure Monitor and Log Analytics, capturing each read or update operation. Alerts can automatically notify security teams or block further requests. Without auditing, silent breaches might persist indefinitely, exposing critical infrastructure.

## Revocation and Cleanup

Ultimately, secrets might reach end-of-life, be replaced, or discovered compromised. Revoking old secrets ensures no unauthorized usage. For example, if a secret is posted accidentally on a public GitHub repo, that secret should be revoked immediately, and a new one generated. This step often aligns with rotation, but typically done on-demand for urgent incidents. Cleanly removing secrets once they are no longer needed helps avoid stale credentials lurking in code or logs.

Each of these stages builds a layered defense, ensuring that secrets remain confidential, only authorized consumers retrieve them, usage is fully logged, and any compromised or expired secrets become useless quickly. When approached methodically, secrets management significantly shrinks the threat surface for modern applications and reduces the operational friction around rotating, revoking, or distributing credentials.

# Exploring Azure Key Vault

## Overview

Azure Key Vault offers a centralized, cloud-based solution for storing and managing keys, secrets, and certificates. By integrating with other Azure resources, it delivers uniform access controls and detailed logging. A typical use case is an application needing a database password: Instead of embedding credentials in code or environment variables, the application retrieves them at runtime from Key Vault. This practice keeps credentials out of source control, fosters dynamic secret usage, and ensures each environment references the same secure store. In addition, Key Vault supports hardware security modules (HSM) for advanced cryptographic operations and compliance standards.

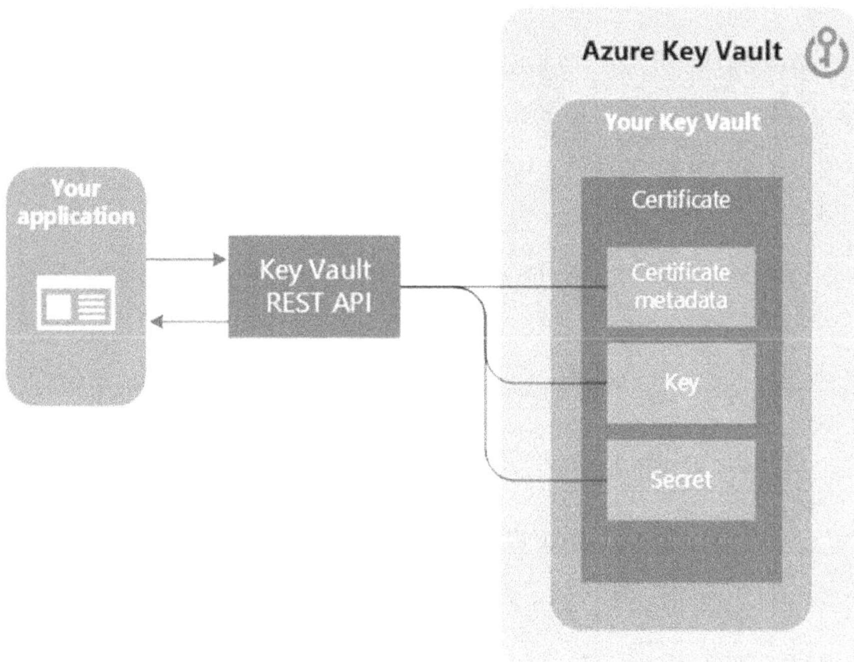


**Fig 7.2 Microsoft Azure Key Vault**

## Key Vault Setup and Policies

The journey starts with creating a vault in a resource group, specifying attributes like location, tenant ID, and SKU as below:

```
resource "azurerm_key_vault" "demo_vault" {
  name                       = "exampleKeyVault"
  location                   = azurerm_resource_group.demo.location
  resource_group_name = azurerm_resource_group.demo.name
  tenant_id                  =
data.azurerm_client_config.current.tenant_id
  sku_name                   = "standard"
  soft_delete_retention_days = 14
}
```

In the above, you define whether soft delete or purge protection is enabled, controlling how quickly secrets can be permanently removed.

Next, you refine access by adding policies:

```
resource "azurerm_key_vault_access_policy" "demo_policy" {
  key_vault_id = azurerm_key_vault.demo_vault.id
  tenant_id    = data.azurerm_client_config.current.tenant_id
  object_id    = data.azurerm_client_config.current.object_id
  secret_permissions = ["get", "set", "delete", "list"]
}
```

This grants get, set, delete, and list capabilities to the current principal, enabling them to manipulate secrets. Always limit roles to only those necessary. If an application only needs read access, do not grant it the ability to delete or update secrets.

## Creating and Managing Secrets

Once policies exist, secrets can be stored. For instance:

```
resource "azurerm_key_vault_secret" "db_secret" {
  name         = "db-password"
  value        = "supersecure123!"
  key_vault_id = azurerm_key_vault.demo_vault.id
```

```
}
```

The secret is then accessible to any principal with "get" permissions. If you want to integrate this with an Azure SQL Server definition, retrieve the secret at plan/apply time via a data block:

```
data "azurerm_key_vault_secret" "db_password_lookup" {
  name         = "db-password"
  key_vault_id = azurerm_key_vault.demo_vault.id
}
```

Now, the data.azurerm_key_vault_secret.db_password_lookup.value can supply credentials for another resource. This approach ensures that your .tf files do not hardcode passwords. Additionally, secrets in Key Vault can be versioned, so rotating them does not break references. You can switch to the newest version for sure.

## Integrations and Usage Patterns

Azure Key Vault extends beyond static secrets. It can store encryption keys for server-side encryption, sign or verify data with HSM-protected keys, and manage SSL certificates for web apps. Terraform can manage these items similarly, creating or rotating them. Many Azure services natively connect with Key Vault. For example, Azure Functions can read environment variables from a vault reference, or Azure Kubernetes Service can reference secrets from Key Vault for container environment variables. This fosters a principle of never storing sensitive data in plain text or ephemeral files. While these integrations reduce friction, you must confirm that each service's managed identity or principal is authorized.

## Rotating, Auditing, and Monitoring

Key Vault logs each secret retrieval, enabling auditing. A recommended practice is hooking Key Vault to a Log Analytics workspace. That captures events like secret read or update. Administrators can then set alerts if unusual secret reads spike. For rotation, you can define expiration dates or let an external script automatically refresh secrets, updating the value in Key Vault. Consumers that read secrets on each startup then naturally pick up the new credentials. If the old version remains accessible, you can schedule its removal after a grace period. This strategy helps keep compromised secrets from lingering indefinitely.

## Sample Program: Referencing DB Password

Imagine a scenario: You maintain an app referencing a MySQL password in Key Vault. The entire .tf code might do something like this:

```
resource "azurerm_key_vault_secret" "mysql_pass" {
```

```
  name         = "mysql-password"
  key_vault_id = azurerm_key_vault.demo_vault.id
  value        = "P@ssw0rd123"
  tags = {
    environment = "production"
  }
}
data "azurerm_key_vault_secret" "lookup_mysql_pass" {
  name         = azurerm_key_vault_secret.mysql_pass.name
  key_vault_id = azurerm_key_vault.demo_vault.id
}
resource "azurerm_mysql_server" "my_db" {
  name                = "myprodserver"
  resource_group_name = azurerm_resource_group.demo.name
  location            = azurerm_resource_group.demo.location
  version             = "5.7"
  administrator_login          = "dbadmin"
  administrator_login_password =
data.azurerm_key_vault_secret.lookup_mysql_pass.value
  sku_name = "B_Gen5_2"
}
```

In the above, the password is safely stored in Key Vault, invisible to your main code. The MySQL server resource retrieves it dynamically. If your security team decides to rotate the password monthly, simply updating the secret or rotating it at Key Vault's side will ensure that next time you run Terraform or redeploy, you adopt the new password.

# Managing Secrets

Let us say we have an application that requires database credentials. These credentials are considered sensitive information and shouldn't be stored directly in the Terraform code. Instead, we're going to securely store them in Azure Key Vault and access them when needed.

First, we need to configure the Azure provider and set up the Azure Key Vault resource as below:

```
provider "azurerm" {
  features {}
}
data "azurerm_client_config" "current" {}
resource "azurerm_resource_group" "example" {
  name     = "example-resources"
  location = "West Europe"
}
resource "azurerm_key_vault" "example" {
  name                        = "examplekeyvault"
  location                    =
azurerm_resource_group.example.location
  resource_group_name         =
azurerm_resource_group.example.name
  enabled_for_disk_encryption = true
  tenant_id                   =
data.azurerm_client_config.current.tenant_id
  soft_delete_retention_days  = 7
  purge_protection_enabled    = false
  sku_name                    = "standard"
}
```

Here, we have set up the provider, retrieved the current client configuration, defined a resource group, and set up the Azure Key Vault. We have enabled soft delete and set the retention days to 7.

Next, we need to create access policies for the Key Vault:

```
resource "azurerm_key_vault_access_policy" "example" {
  key_vault_id = azurerm_key_vault.example.id
  tenant_id = data.azurerm_client_config.current.tenant_id
  object_id = data.azurerm_client_config.current.object_id
```

```
  key_permissions = [
     "get",
     "list"
  ]
  secret_permissions = [
     "get",
     "set",
     "delete",
     "list",
  ]
}
```

In the above demonstration, we have given the current client permissions to get, set, delete, and list the secrets.

Now, let us store the database credentials as secrets in Azure Key Vault:

```
resource "azurerm_key_vault_secret" "db_username" {
  name         = "db-username"
  value        = "myusername"
  key_vault_id = azurerm_key_vault.example.id
}
resource "azurerm_key_vault_secret" "db_password" {
  name         = "db-password"
  value        = "mypassword"
  key_vault_id = azurerm_key_vault.example.id
}
```

In this block, we're creating two secrets: db-username and db-password, and storing them in the Azure Key Vault.

Now, let us say we have a Terraform configuration for an Azure SQL Database. We can use the azurerm_key_vault_secret data source to access the secrets:

```
data "azurerm_key_vault_secret" "db_username" {
```

```
  name         = "db-username"
  key_vault_id = azurerm_key_vault.example.id
}
data "azurerm_key_vault_secret" "db_password" {
  name         = "db-password"
  key_vault_id = azurerm_key_vault.example.id
}
resource "azurerm_sql_server" "example" {
  name                         = "mysqlserver"
  resource_group_name          =
azurerm_resource_group.example.name
  location                     =
azurerm_resource_group.example.location
  version                      = "12.0"
  administrator_login          =
data.azurerm_key_vault_secret.db_username.value
  administrator_login_password =
data.azurerm_key_vault_secret.db_password.value
}
```

In this block, we're retrieving the db-username and db-password secrets from the Azure Key Vault and using them to set up the SQL server. If you have multiple environments (e.g., development, staging, production), you might need to create different Key Vaults or secrets for each environment.

# Monitoring and Logging Secrets

The ability to monitor and log access to secrets is vital for maintaining the security and integrity of the systems. Azure Key Vault integrates with Azure Monitor and Azure Log Analytics, offering you the ability to view logs and set up alerts based on specific conditions. This way, you can keep an eye on who is accessing the secrets and when they're doing it. With Terraform, you can manage and configure these settings programmatically.

To begin with, let us make sure that Azure Key Vault is configured to log events. We will need to create a Diagnostic Setting for our Key Vault. In this setting, we will specify that we want to send our logs to a Log Analytics workspace as below:

```
resource "azurerm_log_analytics_workspace" "example" {
  name                = "exampleworkspace"
  location            = azurerm_resource_group.example.location
  resource_group_name = azurerm_resource_group.example.name
  sku                 = "PerGB2018"
  retention_in_days   = 30
}
resource "azurerm_monitor_diagnostic_setting" "example" {
  name                       = "example"
  target_resource_id         = azurerm_key_vault.example.id
  log_analytics_workspace_id =
azurerm_log_analytics_workspace.example.id
  log {
     category = "AuditEvent"
     enabled  = true
     retention_policy {
     enabled = true
     days = 7
     }
  }
  metric {
     category = "AllMetrics"
     retention_policy {
     enabled = true
     days = 7
     }
  }
}
```

In the above given program, we've created a Log Analytics workspace with a 30-day retention policy. We then created a Diagnostic Setting for our Key Vault to send "AuditEvent" logs and "AllMetrics" to the Log Analytics workspace with a 7-day retention policy. The "AuditEvent" logs will capture any event related to the access and usage of the secrets, like the retrieval of a secret, while "AllMetrics" will capture performance metrics. Depending on the needs, you might want to adjust the categories and retention days.

With the logs in place, you can now use Azure Monitor to create alerts based on certain conditions. For example, you can create an alert when a secret is accessed more than a certain number of times within a specified period. In addition, Azure also provides the Azure Key Vault Activity Log, which records any write operation (PUT, PATCH, DELETE) performed on the Key Vault.

# Summary

In this chapter, we took a look at secrets management, which is a key part of keeping any application secure. We started by understanding what secrets are, why they're important for application architecture, and why secrets management is so important. We also went over the standard process flow of secrets management, highlighting the four crucial stages: generation, storage, access, and rotation. Our exploration took us to Azure Key Vault, a robust tool provided by Microsoft Azure to securely store and manage secrets. We covered the initial setup process in a Terraform environment, showing how Azure Key Vault is a centralized, secure, and tightly controlled storage system for secrets.

Finally, we learned how to use Azure Key Vault to manage secrets in a Terraform configuration, with practical demonstrations on how to store, retrieve, and manage secrets. We also learned how to monitor and log secrets access in Azure Key Vault. We also learned how to use Azure Monitor and Azure Log Analytics to view logs, set up alerts, and track secret access. Finally, we walked through a detailed process of implementing monitoring and logging using Terraform, which gives you more security and oversight of secret management.

# CHAPTER 8: ADMINISTERING NETWORKS WITH TERRAFORM

# Networking Overview

In most cloud setups, networking is like the foundation, and a lot of IaC work has to do with building, securing, and maintaining network resources. When using Terraform, you often work with different cloud providers and have to define stuff like subnets, routing, firewalls, load balancers, VPN gateways, and DNS records.If you get the gist of networking, you can make sure your infrastructure deployments stay scalable, secure, and well-structured. Terraform's declarative model, combined with provider-specific resources, allows code-driven administration of such components, but each environment has distinct features, so understanding the universal and provider-specific traits of networking is vital.

Networking typically starts with the notion of an isolated, software-defined environment. In AWS, this is known as a Virtual Private Cloud (VPC), whereas in Azure, it is a Virtual Network (VNet). The idea is basically the same in both: you want to set up a private IP space for your apps and services. You can define a CIDR range, like 10.0.0.0/16, that the environment uses for internal addressing. There is an easy example of Terraform code that specifies the name of the VPC or VNet, its region, and an IP range. Once you've created this environment, it becomes the boundary for subnets, route tables, security groups, and other building blocks.

Subnets are subdivisions within this environment, each subset of IP addresses reserved for a specific use case or set of services. One might place front-end applications in a public subnet so they can receive traffic from the internet, while database services reside in a private subnet that only internal workloads can reach. Terraform requires explicit definitions for each subnet, specifying that it belongs to the overarching environment and inherits the environment's IP range. If a VPC (or VNet) uses 10.0.0.0/16, one subnet might take 10.0.1.0/24, while another uses 10.0.2.0/24. This practice prevents IP collisions and fosters logical separation.

Routing rules direct traffic between subnets or to external destinations. In AWS, route tables define how packets leave the VPC, referencing gateways such as an internet gateway (IGW) for public traffic or a NAT gateway for private traffic to the internet. In Azure, route tables perform a similar role by binding custom routes to subnets. Terraform resources for route management usually point to a target resource—like an IGW's ID or an IP of a firewall device—that acts as next hop. These routing definitions transform a cluster of subnets into a cohesive network where traffic moves logically according to needs.

Security boundaries often rely on network access controls. In AWS, that role is played by security groups and network ACLs, whereas Azure uses network security groups (NSGs) and, optionally, application security groups for higher granularity. Security group rules typically define which inbound and outbound traffic is permitted, referencing protocols, ports, and source/destination addresses. Terraform code spells out each rule, referencing resources that store IP addresses or environment variables for convenience. If the user wants to allow SSH from any IP range or only from a known corporate IP, the security group rule is updated accordingly. By storing these definitions in version control, teams can see how firewall stances change over time.

DNS stands as another critical aspect. Whether the environment requires private DNS resolution among subnets or public resolution for external requests, Terraform can define zones and records. In AWS, the Route 53 service organizes hosted zones, while in Azure, DNS zones exist as separate resources. This approach fosters consistent naming, so you do not manually click around a DNS console to add or edit an A record. Instead, they specify the zone name, subdomain, TTL, and IP address in Terraform. The next plan/apply cycle modifies the DNS configuration automatically. This ensures that DNS and networking remain closely linked, reducing mistakes such as mismatched domain entries or references to stale IP addresses.

Another essential concept for more advanced setups is load balancing. In AWS, one might define an Elastic Load Balancer (ELB) or Application Load Balancer (ALB), and in Azure, an Azure Load Balancer or Application Gateway. Each solution routes incoming traffic from a public endpoint to backend VMs or containers, possibly distributing load and performing health checks. Terraform code usually references the subnets in which the load balancer is placed, the security group or NSG rules that allow inbound traffic, and the backend pools that specify target machines. This arrangement merges with auto-scaling groups or scale sets so that newly launched instances automatically register with the load balancer.

Network peering or bridging is important when linking multiple environments. In AWS, VPC peering allows traffic to flow across distinct VPCs that typically remain isolated. Azure has VNet peering for a similar effect. Terraform resources define references to the two networks that need bridging, plus any route modifications or DNS adjustments. Such peering fosters cross-application communication without exposing those networks publicly. Additionally, site-to-site VPNs or private connectivity might be relevant if on-premises data centers must connect securely to a cloud network. Terraform typically references a virtual gateway or VPN gateway resource, sets tunnel parameters, and references remote IP addresses or endpoint credentials.

Monitoring and logging at the network level are also crucial. Services such as flow logs in AWS or network watcher in Azure can track traffic patterns, identify unwanted traffic, or debug connectivity issues. Terraform resources for enabling these logs define the target storage location, retention periods, and scope. As these logs accumulate, we glean insights into performance and security anomalies. If a particular subnet experiences suspicious inbound traffic, the logs quickly highlight it, letting teams revise security rules or block IP ranges as needed.

One final dimension is that networking can vary with advanced container or orchestration tools. In Kubernetes, for example, one might rely on a CNI plugin or a managed solution that sets up subnets behind the scenes. Even so, the underlying VPC or VNet remains relevant for cluster nodes. Understanding how pods and services map to ephemeral or load-balancer IP addresses is essential for a stable environment. In many cases, Terraform code for EKS or AKS references subnets and security constructs, ensuring the cluster's network integration is consistent with broader policies.

Overall, networking in Terraform is the glue binding resources into a functional, secure environment. Mastering subnets, routing, security, load balancing, and DNS fosters robust architecture that scales. Providers like AWS, Azure, or GCP each have unique resource definitions, but the overarching principles remain consistent: define IP ranges and subnets, control traffic flow via route tables or gateways, secure with firewall constructs, and attach DNS or load-balancing as needed. By capturing all this in Terraform, teams unify the management of networking with the rest of their infrastructure, enabling versioned evolution, consistent replication of environments, and rapid iteration of topology changes.

# Manage VPCs

So, creating and organizing a VPC—or a VNet in Azure—involves defining a block of IP addresses for the whole environment, followed by subnets for different services. Here's a quick example in AWS:

```
resource "aws_vpc" "main" {
  cidr_block = "10.0.0.0/16"
  tags = {
    Name = "MainVPC"
  }
}
```

This block sets up the environment, specifying a 10.0.0.0/16 address space. Next, you define subnets that occupy slices of that space, such as 10.0.1.0/24 for a public subnet, and 10.0.2.0/24 for private instances. A typical program for a public subnet includes:

```
resource "aws_subnet" "public_subnet" {
  vpc_id            = aws_vpc.main.id
  cidr_block        = "10.0.1.0/24"
  availability_zone = "us-west-2a"
  tags = {
    Name = "PublicSubnet"
  }
}
```

Then, to allow internet access, you might attach an internet gateway resource:

```
resource "aws_internet_gateway" "gw" {
  vpc_id = aws_vpc.main.id
  tags = {
```

```
    Name = "MainInternetGateway"
  }
}
```

And you modify the route table so that 0.0.0.0/0 traffic goes through that gateway:

```
resource "aws_route" "default_route" {
  route_table_id         = aws_vpc.main.default_route_table_id
  destination_cidr_block = "0.0.0.0/0"
  gateway_id             = aws_internet_gateway.gw.id
}
```

In Azure, the pattern is similar: define a Virtual Network with a certain address space, carve subnets, and optionally add a public IP or an outbound NAT gateway. Terraform's advantage is that the entire topology, from the broad VPC definition down to the final route or NAT setting, appears in one codebase.

# Manage Subnets and Routing

When creating a virtual network, subdividing it into specific subnets facilitates better organization and tighter control over traffic flow. Each subnet can host different tiers of your application or separate environments for security and clarity. In a scenario with AWS, for instance, you might define a public subnet for external-facing services and a private subnet for backend servers or databases. Terraform code typically references the VPC's ID, a distinct CIDR block for each subnet, and any tags or metadata you wish to attach as shown below:

```
resource "aws_subnet" "public_subnet" {
  vpc_id                  = aws_vpc.main.id
  cidr_block              = "10.0.1.0/24"
  availability_zone       = "us-west-2a"
  map_public_ip_on_launch = true
  tags = {
    Name = "PublicSubnet"
  }
}
```

```
resource "aws_subnet" "private_subnet" {
  vpc_id            = aws_vpc.main.id
  cidr_block        = "10.0.2.0/24"
  availability_zone = "us-west-2b"
  tags = {
    Name = "PrivateSubnet"
  }
}
```

If you set map_public_ip_on_launch = true, newly launched instances in that subnet receive a public IP automatically. Otherwise, they remain private. These subnets share the overall 10.0.0.0/16 range from the VPC, but each occupies a distinct portion so their addresses do not overlap.

The next step is controlling how packets traverse inside and outside the VPC. Terraform resources like aws_route_table define custom routes for the subnets. By default, AWS supplies a main route table, but many users create dedicated route tables for each subnet. For instance, you might ensure the public subnet has a default route to an internet gateway, while the private subnet references a NAT gateway for outbound traffic as shown below:

```
resource "aws_route_table" "public_rt" {
  vpc_id = aws_vpc.main.id
  tags = {
    Name = "PublicRouteTable"
  }
}
resource "aws_route" "public_internet_route" {
  route_table_id         = aws_route_table.public_rt.id
  destination_cidr_block = "0.0.0.0/0"
  gateway_id             = aws_internet_gateway.gw.id
}
resource "aws_route_table_association" "public_assoc" {
  subnet_id      = aws_subnet.public_subnet.id
  route_table_id = aws_route_table.public_rt.id
```

```
}
```

In the above, the route_table_association binds the public subnet to the public route table, which includes a default route pointing to the internet gateway. Instances in that subnet can accept inbound traffic and respond to the internet. Meanwhile, for the private subnet, you might define a second route table referencing a NAT gateway or a virtual private gateway if you want site-to-site connectivity.

In Azure, a similar pattern applies using azurerm_subnet, azurerm_route_table, and azurerm_route resources. Regardless of the provider, subnets logically split the IP space, and custom routes direct the traffic to gateways or endpoints.

# Manage Load Balancers

In AWS, the main resource for a classic load balancer is aws_elb, but more modern patterns use aws_lb, which can configure Application or Network Load Balancers. Terraform code typically references subnets for the load balancer's front-end, security groups to allow traffic on certain ports, and back-end target groups for actual server instances.

For example, an Application Load Balancer in AWS might be defined:

```
resource "aws_lb" "app_lb" {
  name               = "my-app-lb"
  load_balancer_type = "application"
  subnets            = [
    aws_subnet.public_subnet.id,
    aws_subnet.public_subnet2.id
  ]
  security_groups    = [aws_security_group.lb_sg.id]
  tags = {
    Environment = "Production"
  }
}
resource "aws_lb_target_group" "app_tg" {
  name        = "app-tg"
  port        = 80
```

```
  protocol    = "HTTP"
  vpc_id      = aws_vpc.main.id
  target_type = "instance"
}
resource "aws_lb_listener" "app_listener" {
  load_balancer_arn = aws_lb.app_lb.arn
  port              = "80"
  protocol          = "HTTP"
  default_action {
    type             = "forward"
    target_group_arn = aws_lb_target_group.app_tg.arn
  }
}
```

In the above, the load balancer is placed in two public subnets for redundancy. The target group listens on port 80, referencing the VPC. The listener ties the load balancer to the target group so incoming traffic on port 80 is forwarded to the back-end instances.

Next, you might register instances or an auto-scaling group with that target group as below:

```
resource "aws_autoscaling_group" "app_asg" {
  name                 = "asg-app"
  max_size             = 5
  min_size             = 1
  desired_capacity     = 2
  vpc_zone_identifier = [
    aws_subnet.private_subnet.id,
    aws_subnet.private_subnet2.id
  ]
  launch_configuration =
aws_launch_configuration.app_config.name
  tag {
```

```
    key                   = "Name"
    value                 = "MyApp"
    propagate_at_launch = true
  }
  lifecycle {
    create_before_destroy = true
  }
}
resource "aws_lb_target_group_attachment" "asg_tg_attach" {
  target_group_arn = aws_lb_target_group.app_tg.arn
  target_id        = "${each.value.id}"
  port             = 80
  for_each = toset(aws_autoscaling_group.app_asg.instance_ids)
}
```

This above program ensures each instance in the auto-scaling group is attached to the load balancer's target group. As the group scales up or down, Terraform updates attachments, letting newly launched instances receive traffic.

In Azure, a similar approach uses azurerm_lb, azurerm_lb_backend_address_pool, and azurerm_lb_probe for health checks. The front-end IP configuration references a public IP or subnet, while rules define which ports forward to the back-end pool. Whether AWS, Azure, or another cloud, load balancers require specifying subnets or IPs for front-end traffic, plus the resources or IPs for back-end traffic.

# Network Configuration Troubleshooting

Errors in Terraform's messages can be super helpful when you're trying to figure out network issues. A lot of the time, they'll point you to missing required parameters, resources that can't be found, or values that are outside the allowed range.

Now, let's dive into some of the common problems and how to fix them when working with Terraform and network configurations:

## Missing Required Parameters

Many Terraform resources have required arguments that must be set for the resource to be created successfully. Omitting a required argument will lead to errors when trying to apply the configuration.

For example, creating an Azure network security group without specifying the location:

```
resource "azurerm_network_security_group" "example" {
# Location is missing
}
```

Running apply would show an error:

```
Error: Missing required argument
```

This occurs because the Azure provider requires the location argument when creating a network security group. Now, if you want to fix it, then it involves:

- Checking provider documentation for which arguments are required
- Specifying all required arguments in the resource configuration
- Running validate and plan to catch missing arguments early

These arguments are like settings that customize the resource, and omitting them is usually because people are either copying and pasting configs or don't know much about the resource arguments.

## Incorrect Resource References

One common mistake when authoring Terraform configurations is attempting to reference a resource that has not been declared. For example, when defining an Azure subnet resource, we may accidentally misspell the name of the virtual network we want to attach it to:

```
resource "azurerm_subnet" "example" {
  virtual_network_name = azurerm_virtual_network.exampl.name
}
```

In the above snippet, we have a typo in the virtual network resource name ("exampl" instead of "example"). When applying this config, Terraform will raise an error:

```
Error: Resource not declared
```

This error occurs because Terraform cannot find the resource being referenced since the name contains a mistake. The solution is to double check that all resource names referenced in the configuration match declared names exactly.

To add more info to you, the common sources of this issue include:

- Misspelled resource names
- Forgetting to define a resource being referenced
- Accidentally referencing the wrong resource entirely

## Overlapping CIDR Blocks

If you define network resources like subnets or VPCs with overlapping CIDR blocks, you'll get errors when you provision the infrastructure. For example, if two subnets within the same VPC are assigned address spaces that overlap:

```
resource "azurerm_subnet" "subnet1" {
  address_prefix = "10.0.0.0/16"
}
resource "azurerm_subnet" "subnet2" {
  address_prefix = "10.0.0.0/24"
}
```

The second subnet overlaps with the first. Applying this Terraform will fail with an error:

```
Error: CIDR blocks overlap
```

Now to resolve, the CIDR blocks must be disjoint with following ways to achieve:

- Adjust the prefixes to not overlap (e.g. 10.0.0.0/16 and 10.1.0.0/24)
- Create a variable for the VPC CIDR and derive non-overlapping subnet CIDRs
- Use the cidrsubnet() function to automatically partition VPC space
- Validate CIDRs don't overlap using validation tools like OPA

In all these cases, **terraform validate** and **terraform plan** are your best friends. Run these commands before applying changes to catch errors early. And don't forget to use terraform fmt and terraform taint to format the configuration and recreate resources, respectively. Keep in mind that recreating resources could lead to downtime for production services.

# Summary

The first half of this chapter covered the foundations of networking in Terraform. The first thing that we concentrated on was virtual private clouds, often known as VPCs. After getting a handle on virtual private clouds (VPCs), we switched our focus to the management of subnets and routing. We went over how to set up routing tables and rules to manage network traffic, as well as how to construct subnets inside of a virtual private cloud (VPC). Additionally, we investigated the DNS administration features of Terraform and learned how it may assist in the maintenance of DNS records and zones.

In the final part of our chapter, we dug into more difficult topics such as the management of load balancers and the automated scaling of resources. We studied how to auto-scale resources depending on a set of parameters, and we learned about how to use Terraform to design and operate load balancers. When it comes to working with Terraform and network setups, we also brought attention to the significance of troubleshooting and learned common problems along with the remedies to those problems. We addressed how to identify and resolve common issues such as missing needed parameters, erroneous references to other resources and overlapping CIDR blocks. These issues can be caused by a variety of things, including missing essential parameters.

# CHAPTER 9: ADVANCED TOPICS IN TERRAFORM

This chapter is really important because it's designed to tackle the tricky parts and clear up any confusion. At the start of this chapter, we're going to dive into the different types of errors you might run into when working with Terraform. We'll break them down into three categories: syntax, semantic, and runtime errors. We'll go deep into these error types, show you real-world examples, and offer full solutions. Then, we'll explore ways to boost the performance of your Terraform operations by keeping an eye on and tweaking key performance indicators like execution time, resource usage, and code efficiency.

Another important thing we'll learn in this chapter is how to import pre-provisioned infrastructure into Terraform. We know how important it is to work with existing resources, so we'll give you specific instructions on importing Azure resources. You'll see how you can easily bring already provisioned infrastructure under Terraform's management. And we'll spend a lot of time talking about testing in Terraform. We'll go over four main types of testing: unit testing, integration testing, validation testing, and compliance testing. We'll show you some examples to help you understand the unique value each type of testing provides and how it contributes to the reliability of your infrastructure.

# Categories of Errors

While working with Terraform, you will unavoidably encounter errors, which can be broadly categorized into syntax errors, semantic errors, and runtime errors. Each type comes up at a different point in the Terraform workflow, so you'll need to use a different troubleshooting strategy for each one.

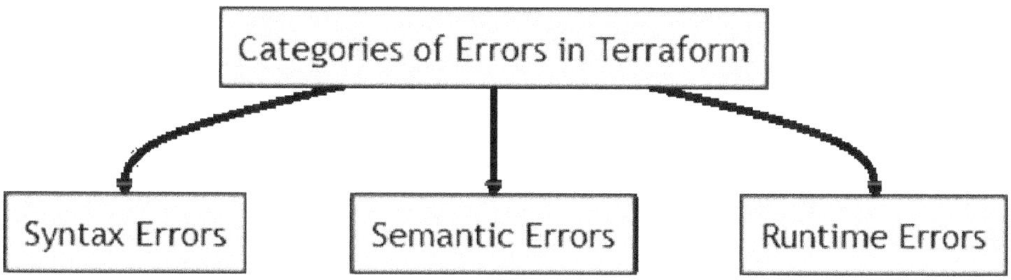


**Fig 9.1 Error Types in Terraform**

- **Syntax Errors**: This error occurs when the Terraform code fails to conform to the Terraform language's structure. Examples include unclosed braces, misspelled keywords, or invalid operators. The **`terraform validate`** command often flags syntax issues, and error messages typically highlight exactly where Terraform's parser failed.
- **Semantic Errors**: These happens when the code is syntactically correct but references or logic are incorrect. For instance, referencing a resource that doesn't exist, specifying a resource property with invalid data types, or providing a subnet block outside the parent VPC's CIDR. Though no syntax mistake is made,

Terraform's plan/apply process catches these logic flaws.

- **Runtime Errors**: These types of errors emerge when the code is valid, but issues arise during resource creation or updates. Common causes include API rate limits, permission denials, or ephemeral network hiccups. These errors show up once Terraform communicates with the cloud provider. They may also involve mismatches in Terraform state – for instance, if the resource was changed externally but not updated in Terraform, leading to drift.

Besides these three, a set of specialized errors may revolve around concurrency in multi-user environments, state lock problems, or partial failures when certain steps succeed but others do not. Resolving these typically involves revisiting how the environment is structured, ensuring robust usage of remote state, or adjusting the concurrency approach in a CI/CD pipeline.

# Troubleshooting Syntax Errors

Syntax errors in Terraform are the easiest to spot because they prevent the code from parsing altogether. Typical examples include missing braces, typos in resource blocks, or misusing operators. While they're often straightforward to fix, they can be frustrating if the error message doesn't align neatly with your code's structure. Below is an illustration of a missing brace:

```
resource "azurerm_resource_group" "example"
  name     = "example-rg"
  location = "West Europe"
}
```

Without the opening brace after the resource declaration, Terraform fails to parse the block. So if you run **`terraform validate`** or terraform plan, it might produce an error like:

```
Error: Missing '{'
  on main.tf line 2, in resource "azurerm_resource_group"
"example":
   2: resource "azurerm_resource_group" "example"
Blocks must be enclosed by '{' and '}'.
```

Once you add the missing brace:

```
resource "azurerm_resource_group" "example" {
  name     = "example-rg"
```

```
  location = "West Europe"
}
```

the code parses correctly.

Another syntax pitfall arises when substituting the wrong character or ignoring required punctuation. For instance, incorrectly using colon (:) where Terraform expects an equals sign (=) can break your code in earlier Terraform versions, or vice versa in older HCL syntax. Relying on a code editor that supports Terraform syntax highlighting—such as Visual Studio Code with the HashiCorp Terraform extension—prevents many of these slipups. These tools often underline suspicious code blocks and provide linting suggestions.

For more advanced detection of syntax-level missteps, the terraform fmt and **terraform validate** commands are invaluable. The former auto-formats your code to conform with best practices, sometimes revealing subtle typos, while the latter checks the code's structure.

# Troubleshooting Semantic Errors

A semantic error is when your Terraform code is technically correct, but there's a logical or contextual mismatch that stops it from working right. The following program illustrate common semantic issues and how to fix them.

## Example 1: Referencing Nonexistent Resource

Suppose you want to attach a subnet to a route table but accidentally reference the wrong name for the route table. Below is the flawed code:

```
resource "azurerm_virtual_network" "vnet_main" {
  name                = "vnet-main"
  location            = azurerm_resource_group.rg.location
  resource_group_name = azurerm_resource_group.rg.name
  address_space       = ["10.0.0.0/16"]
}
resource "azurerm_subnet" "subnet_app" {
  name                 = "subnet-app"
  resource_group_name  = azurerm_resource_group.rg.name
  virtual_network_name =
azurerm_virtual_network.vnet_main.name
```

```
  address_prefixes     = ["10.0.1.0/24"]
}
# This route table is named "route_main"
resource "azurerm_route_table" "route_main" {
  name                = "main-rt"
  location            = azurerm_resource_group.rg.location
  resource_group_name = azurerm_resource_group.rg.name
}
# Semantic mistake: referencing "route_table_main" instead of
"route_main"
resource "azurerm_subnet_route_table_association"
"subnet_assoc" {
  subnet_id      = azurerm_subnet.subnet_app.id
  route_table_id = azurerm_route_table.route_table_main.id
}
```

During **terraform plan**, you see an error like:

```
Error: Reference to undeclared resource
  on main.tf line 31, in resource
"azurerm_subnet_route_table_association" "subnet_assoc":
  31:   route_table_id =
azurerm_route_table.route_table_main.id
A managed resource "azurerm_route_table" "route_table_main"
has not been declared...
```

This can be overcome if we fix the resource reference to match the actual resource name as below:

```
resource "azurerm_subnet_route_table_association"
"subnet_assoc" {
  subnet_id      = azurerm_subnet.subnet_app.id
  route_table_id = azurerm_route_table.route_main.id
}
```

## Example 2: Subnet outside VNet Address Space

Let us assume you define a VNet with a CIDR of 10.0.0.0/16 but inadvertently specify a subnet prefix that conflicts with or lies outside that range:

```
resource "azurerm_virtual_network" "vnet_main" {
  name                = "vnet-main"
  location            = azurerm_resource_group.rg.location
  resource_group_name = azurerm_resource_group.rg.name
  address_space       = ["10.0.0.0/16"]
}
# Wrong: 10.1.0.0/24 is outside or not overlapping correctly
resource "azurerm_subnet" "subnet_app" {
  name                 = "subnet-app"
  resource_group_name  = azurerm_resource_group.rg.name
  virtual_network_name =
azurerm_virtual_network.vnet_main.name
  address_prefixes     = ["10.1.0.0/24"]
}
```

If the environment or region mandates that subnets remain within 10.0.0.0/16, **terraform plan** might produce:

```
Error: Subnet's prefix is not within the parent network's
address prefix
```

To fix it, you need to correctly align the subnet with the VNet's range as below:

```
address_prefixes = ["10.0.1.0/24"]
```

## Example 3: Incorrect Data Type for an Argument

There are some resources that expect a list instead of a single string. For instancc, an address_space in a VNet typically demands a list of strings:

```
# Potentially flawed code
```

```
address_space = "10.0.0.0/16"
```

Here, Terraform might complain:

```
Error: Incorrect value type
  on main.tf line 9, in resource "azurerm_virtual_network"
"vnet_main":
   9: address_space = "10.0.0.0/16"
Inappropriate value for attribute "address_space": list of
string required.
```

To fix it up, simply provide a list as below:

```
address_space = ["10.0.0.0/16"]
```

But while you do, you must ensure that your code matches the resource's typed arguments avoids this class of semantic error.

# Troubleshooting Runtime Errors

When an external factor interferes with Terraform's attempt to provision a resource on a provider, a runtime error occurs. Unlike syntax or semantic issues, runtime errors typically indicate provider limitations, insufficient permissions, or transient connectivity issues.

## Example 1: Permission Denied

Imagine you are creating a resource group in Azure with a service principal that lacks permission:

```
resource "azurerm_resource_group" "rg_secure" {
  name     = "rg-secure"
  location = "West Europe"
}
```

During apply, you might see:

```
Error: Error creating Resource Group "rg-secure" (Subscription
"xxxx..."):
AuthorizationFailed: The client 'xxxxxxxx' with object id
'yyyyyyyy' does not have authorization to perform action ...
```

To fix this situation, you ensure that the service principal or user identity has the correct role assignment. Here, you might run:

```
az role assignment create \
  --role Contributor \
  --scope /subscriptions/... \
  --assignee <object_id or principal_id>
```

Then re-run **terraform apply** and check the provider logs or using the Azure portal's Activity Log can confirm the missing permission.

## Example 2: Cloud Resource Not Available in a Chosen Region

If you specify a VM size or a feature that is not offered in the region, Terraform might fail with a "BadRequest" or "InvalidParameter" error:

```
resource "azurerm_linux_virtual_machine" "vm_rare" {
  name                   = "rare-vm"
  location               = "West Europe"
  resource_group_name    = azurerm_resource_group.rg.name
  size                   = "Standard_E64i_v3"  # Suppose it's
unavailable in this region
  # Additional config ...
}
```

Terraform returns something like:

```
Error: Code="InvalidParameter" Message="The requested size is
currently not available in location 'West Europe' for
subscription..."
```

Now to fix this up, simply choose a size valid in West Europe or pick another region:

```
size = "Standard_DS1_v2"
```

or

```
location = "East US"
```

Then type **az vm list-skus** to see which SKUs are valid in a region.

## Example 3: API Rate Limits

Sometimes, the creation of many resources quickly can lead to throttling:

```
Error: network.SecurityRulesClient#CreateOrUpdate: Failure
responding to request:
StatusCode=429 -- Original Error: Code="TooManyRequests"
Message="The server returned too many requests for this
subscription."
```

So here, we need to slowdown or do batch resource creation. In large deployments, you might break them into multiple steps or rely on Terraform's parallelism settings:

```
terraform apply -parallelism=5
```

Alternatively, re-run after some delay, or consider using less concurrency.

## Example 4: NAT Gateway Not Fully Created

There are scenarios when you define a NAT gateway or route that depends on a newly created resource. If Terraform tries to associate the route prematurely, you get partial success. For instance:

```
resource "aws_nat_gateway" "nat" {
  allocation_id = aws_eip.nat.id
  subnet_id     = aws_subnet.public_subnet.id
}
resource "aws_route" "private_internet_route" {
  route_table_id         = aws_route_table.private_rt.id
  destination_cidr_block = "0.0.0.0/0"
  nat_gateway_id         = aws_nat_gateway.nat.id
}
```

Should the NAT gateway take extra time to allocate an IP, the route creation might fail. A runtime error indicates it cannot find the NAT gateway in the expected state.

Now to fix this, usually, Terraform's internal dependency graph handles creation order. But if the NAT resource or EIP is slow, re-running **terraform apply** after a short wait often works.

If necessary, you can define explicit depends_on:

```
resource "aws_route" "private_internet_route" {
  route_table_id         = aws_route_table.private_rt.id
  destination_cidr_block = "0.0.0.0/0"
  nat_gateway_id         = aws_nat_gateway.nat.id
  depends_on = [
    aws_nat_gateway.nat
  ]
}
```

This ensures Terraform never tries to create the route before the NAT gateway fully exists.

## Example 5: Resource Drift

If a coworker changes the resource in the cloud console, Terraform's state may no longer match reality. The next **`terraform apply`** might fail, or it might produce unexpected changes. A typical sign is an error that the resource is "inconsistent with the state."

To fix this, just re-import the resource if it still exists, or remove references from Terraform if it is intentionally removed externally. For re-import, define the resource in code, then run:

```
terraform import azurerm_virtual_machine.vm_rare
"/subscriptions/.../resourceGroups/.../providers/Microsoft.Com
pute/virtualMachines/rare-vm"
```

You may check the plan to confirm alignment. If the resource was removed, delete the Terraform references to avoid future conflicts.

By systematically reading error messages, verifying resource definitions, verifying region or permissions constraints, and re-checking references, you can tackle nearly all runtime issues. Often, the best approach is to parse the exact error from the provider's API—whether it's a 403 for insufficient rights, a 429 for throttling, or a 404 for missing resources—then rectify your environment, code, or sequence accordingly.

# Terraform Performance Indicators (KPI)

There are both subjective and objective ways to measure and optimize terraform performance. Subjectively, you might notice that a typical Terraform application is taking too long or that the pipeline is repeatedly hitting cloud provider limits. Objectively, you can monitor key performance indicators (KPIs) to identify areas for improvement, reduce operational costs, and streamline infrastructure changes.

Typically, several KPIs emerge as critical:

## Execution Speed

This measures how long Terraform needs to complete a plan and apply cycle. A large environment with hundreds of resources can lengthen these steps, especially if many of them are in the same module or if certain resources block parallel creation. The duration often depends on cloud APIs, concurrency settings, and resource complexity.

For example, a single AWS VPC plus multiple subnets and route tables might apply quickly, but adding 50 EC2 instances across multiple subnets with security groups can push the cycle longer. One way to speed it up is by using **`-parallelism`** to tune how many resources Terraform tries to create at once:

```
terraform apply -parallelism=10
```

In a normal environment, 10 concurrent operations might be safe, but overly high concurrency risks hitting API throttles. Another approach is a modular design so that fewer resources are in the same module, letting you create them in smaller, more manageable groups.

## Resource Utilization

While Terraform itself typically does not consume massive CPU or memory on the local machine, the real concern is the overhead on the infrastructure. For example, if you maintain ephemeral environments that spin up large clusters, you risk ballooning costs. Monitoring how many resources Terraform regularly spawns – and how long they remain – ensures you do not overpay for short-lived or underused services. Tools like AWS Cost Explorer or Azure Monitor show usage and costs for each resource. If usage is low or ephemeral, consider adjusting the config to spin down resources more aggressively or only at certain pipeline stages.

## Error Rates

A codebase that frequently triggers errors or partial applies indicates deeper issues. High error frequency might mean misalignment with the cloud provider, concurrency issues, or invalid resource definitions. Tracking how often **`terraform apply`** fails and categorizing those failures – syntax, semantic, or runtime – helps determine if you need improved code review, environment readiness checks, or provider policies. When user or pipeline logs fill with repeated "429 TooManyRequests," your solution may be to either reduce parallel operations or upgrade your account's API quotas.

## Maintainability

This KPI looks at how easily the Terraform code can be adapted, extended, or debugged. Indicators include the ratio of repeated blocks, how many resources reside in a single file, and whether modules are used appropriately. Overly monolithic .tf files hamper collaboration and raise confusion for new team members. Conversely, well-structured modules with clear variable definitions reduce duplication. Tools like **`tflint`** or **`tfsec`** can check for code consistency and security best practices. Meanwhile, "how quickly can we add a new subnet or scale the cluster?" is a real-world measure of maintainability.

## Deployment Frequency and Lead Time

These DevOps-oriented KPIs assess how often and how rapidly the team can push changes to production. If an infrastructure update (e.g., adding a new VM or changing a security rule) takes days to go from commit to deployment, your pipeline may be unoptimized or risk-averse. A faster lead time, in hours or even minutes, means agile iteration on infrastructure is feasible without incurring heavy overhead. This usually pairs with robust testing, so you do not sacrifice stability for speed.

Now =to improve these KPIs, we need to refine your Terraform configuration. For execution speed, tune concurrency or break large deployments into smaller modules. For resource usage, carefully define ephemeral resource lifecycles or adopt cost-effective cloud usage patterns (like shutting down dev environments during off hours). The reduction in the error rates often means better code review processes, local validation steps (**`terraform validate`**, **`terraform plan`**) in CI, and using proven modules. And finally, ensuring your pipeline is fully automated – from linting to plan to apply – speeds up deployment frequency and lowers lead time.

# Import Existing Infrastructure

Terraform can import existing resources that were created manually or by another tool, allowing you to bring them under Terraform's control without re-creating them. This makes it easier to manage legacy or pre-provisioned infrastructure going forward. The general approach is:

- First to write a Terraform resource block describing the resource.
- Then run **terraform import <resource_address> <actual_resource_id>**. Here, the Terraform reads the real resource data from the provider's API, merges it into state, and confirms a successful match.

Below is an example illustrating to import an existing Resource Group:

### *Write Terraform Resource*

Suppose you have a resource group named **`my-existing-rg`** in the **`East US`** location. For this, you create a resource block in your **`main.tf`**:

```
provider "azurerm" {
  features {}
}
resource "azurerm_resource_group" "existing_rg" {
  name     = "my-existing-rg"
  location = "East US"
}
```

### *Find Resource ID*

You need the actual Azure resource ID. With Azure CLI:

```
az group show --name my-existing-rg --query id --output tsv
```

It outputs something like:

```
/subscriptions/00000000-1111-2222-3333-
444444444444/resourceGroups/my-existing-rg
```

### *Run Import Command*

Then use that ID when importing:

```
terraform init
terraform import azurerm_resource_group.existing_rg
"/subscriptions/00000000-1111-2222-3333-
444444444444/resourceGroups/my-existing-rg"
```

Terraform fetches the current resource data from Azure and compares it with your written configuration. If it aligns, the resource is now in Terraform's state. If your code lacks required properties or has mismatched data (e.g., you wrote location = "West US" but the resource is in East US), import fails or warns of drift. Adjust your .tf code to precisely match the real resource's properties, then re-run.

### *Confirm with Plan*

After import, run:

```
terraform plan
```

Terraform shows "No changes," indicating the resource in state matches your code's resource block. If the plan includes changes, you either accept them (if you intentionally want to override some properties) or tweak your code to reflect the actual resource.

If you must import dozens or hundreds of resources, the manual approach can be tedious. You might rely on partial automation or third-party tools like **`terraformer`** (by Google Cloud) to generate resource blocks from the existing environment. However, since each resource in Terraform typically requires a resource block matching the real resource configuration, you typically must ensure correctness. Once imported, you can apply changes to those resources as normal.

If your environment already has partially Terraform-managed resources, ensure that your resource blocks do not inadvertently overlap. For instance, if you want to import a subnet that is now included in another module, you risk collisions in state. Checking the current resources in your state with **`terraform state list`** helps see if a resource is already known. If it is, you skip import. If not, define the resource, import, and unify everything in the code to maintain consistency.

# Executing Unit Testing

Unit testing in the Terraform world is about validating the behavior of an isolated component—often a module or a single resource—without involving a larger environment. The primary goal is to ensure that given certain inputs (variables), the **`Terraform plan`** produces the desired configuration. One popular approach is using Terratest, a Go library enabling automated tests for Terraform.

Below is an example showing how to set up and run a basic unit test with Terratest. For this let us assume we have a Terraform module / configuration that creates a resource group and an Azure Storage Account.

Given below is a minimal **`main.tf`**:

```
provider "azurerm" {
  features {}
}
variable "resource_group_name" {
  type        = string
  description = "Name for the resource group."
}
variable "storage_account_name" {
```

```
  type        = string
  description = "Name for the storage account."
}
resource "azurerm_resource_group" "rg" {
  name     = var.resource_group_name
  location = "East US"
}
resource "azurerm_storage_account" "acct" {
  name                     = var.storage_account_name
  resource_group_name      = azurerm_resource_group.rg.name
  location                 =
azurerm_resource_group.rg.location
  account_tier             = "Standard"
  account_replication_type = "LRS"
}
output "storage_id" {
  value = azurerm_storage_account.acct.id
}
```

In the above, we expect to pass in two variables: **resource_group_name** and **storage_account_name**. Terraform will create a Resource Group and a Storage Account, then output the storage account's ID.

In **test/unit_test.go**, you write your Terratest code:package test

```
import (
    "fmt"
    "testing"
    "github.com/gruntwork-io/terratest/modules/terraform"
    "github.com/stretchr/testify/assert"
)
func TestStorageAccountUnit(t *testing.T) {
```

```
    t.Parallel()
    // Define variables for Terraform
    rgName := "test-rg"
    storageName := "teststoracctxyz"
    // Configure Terratest options
    terraformOptions := &terraform.Options{
        // Path to our Terraform folder
        TerraformDir: "../",
        Vars: map[string]interface{}{
            "resource_group_name":  rgName,
            "storage_account_name": storageName,
        },
    }
    // Run `terraform init` and `terraform apply`. Fail if any
errors.
    defer terraform.Destroy(t, terraformOptions)
    terraform.InitAndApply(t, terraformOptions)
    // Retrieve outputs
    storageID := terraform.Output(t, terraformOptions,
"storage_id")
    // Verify outputs with simple checks
    // We just check that storage_id is not empty, or you can
do more advanced checks
    assert.NotEmpty(t, storageID, "Storage ID should not be
empty")
    // Optionally, verify the storage name we set is reflected
in the ID, if the pattern matches
    expected := fmt.Sprintf("teststoracctxyz")
    assert.Contains(t, storageID, expected, "Storage ID should
contain the provided storage account name")
}
```

Here,

- **terraformOptions** points to the parent directory and sets up the variables **`resource_group_name`** and **`storage_account_name`**.
- **defer terraform.Destroy(...)** ensures that after the test completes, Terraform destroys the resources it created. This keeps costs low and avoids leaving test infrastructure behind.
- **terraform.InitAndApply(...)** runs **`terraform init`** followed by **`terraform apply`** with the specified variables.
- **terraform.Output** fetches the value of **`storage_id`** from the configuration's output block.
- And, we use **assert** from **`testify`** to check that the output is non-empty, and optionally confirm it matches an expected pattern.

From the **`test`** directory, run:

```
go mod init github.com/youruser/yourrepo

go get github.com/gruntwork-io/terratest/modules/terraform

go get github.com/stretchr/testify

go test -v
```

This process initializes a Go module, retrieves Terratest and testify dependencies, and then executes the test. If successful, you see logs indicating that Terraform applied successfully and that all assertions passed. If it fails, logs then instruct you to whether it was a resource creation issue or an unexpected output.

We're only verifying this small module's behavior with minimal external integration. We do not connect multiple modules or major environment dependencies. The result is a simpler, faster test focusing on one piece of logic—e.g., verifying that it can create a resource group and storage account, that the plan or output is as expected, etc.

# Implementing Integration Testing

In integration testing, you check how multiple modules or components work together. Instead of checking the correctness of a single resource, you ensure that the modules work together cohesively-for example, a virtual network module plus a virtual machine module plus some network security rules. The idea is to catch problems that arise only when multiple parts have to coordinate resource references, outputs, or dependencies.

For example, let us say, we have:

- A **vnet_module** that creates a Virtual Network and a Subnet.
- A **vm_module** that spins up a VM referencing that VNet's subnet.

- Potentially a **nsg_module** for security group rules.

Your code references these modules in a top-level **`main.tf`**:

```
module "vnet_module" {
  source = "./modules/vnet_module"
  vnet_name = "integration-vnet"
  cidr_block = "10.0.0.0/16"
  subnet_cidr = "10.0.1.0/24"
}
module "vm_module" {
  source = "./modules/vm_module"
  vm_name = "int-test-vm"
  subnet_id = module.vnet_module.subnet_id
  # other variables...
}
```

In test/integration_test.go, we run the following:

```
package test
import (
    "testing"
    "github.com/gruntwork-io/terratest/modules/terraform"
    "github.com/stretchr/testify/assert"
)
func TestIntegrationModules(t *testing.T) {
    t.Parallel()
    // Variables for the test
    vnetName := "integration-vnet"
    vmName := "int-test-vm"
    // Terratest config
    terraformOptions := &terraform.Options{
```

```
        TerraformDir: "../",
        Vars: map[string]interface{}{
            "vnet_name": vnetName,
            "vm_name":   vmName,
        },
    }
    // Ensure cleanup after test
    defer terraform.Destroy(t, terraformOptions)
    // Deploy
    terraform.InitAndApply(t, terraformOptions)
    // Retrieve outputs
    actualVnetID := terraform.Output(t, terraformOptions,
"vnet_id")
    actualSubnetID := terraform.Output(t, terraformOptions,
"subnet_id")
    actualVMID := terraform.Output(t, terraformOptions,
"vm_id")
    // Confirm they are non-empty
    assert.NotEmpty(t, actualVnetID, "VNet ID should be set")
    assert.NotEmpty(t, actualSubnetID, "Subnet ID should be
set")
    assert.NotEmpty(t, actualVMID, "VM ID should be set")
    // Additional checks:
    // e.g., If you have a module output that references the
subnet or NSG name, verify the string or pattern
}
```

Here in the above,

- We define variables for the integration test – a VNet name, a VM name, etc.
- We set these in **Vars** for **`terraformOptions`** so they override any default.
- **InitAndApply** runs, creating the entire stack: the VNet, the Subnet, and the VM.
- We retrieve relevant outputs, such as vnet_id, subnet_id, or vm_id, which might come

from either the modules or top-level code. If all these IDs are valid, it suggests the modules integrated properly.

An integration test might fail if, for example, the VM expects a subnet_id, but the output of the vnet_module is misspelled (resulting in a semantic error). Alternatively, a concurrency problem or a missing depends_on could cause a partial build. The Terratest logs will show whether the plan or apply step caused the error. If it's a missing reference, fix your module code. If it's a concurrency or region issue, fix the environment or application logic.

While both unit and integration testing use the same Terratest fundamentals, the difference lies in scope and complexity. Unit tests quickly confirm small code segments work as planned, while integration tests see if modules play nicely together.

# Running Validation Testing

Validation testing focuses on assessing whether the final deployed infrastructure behaves as intended in a live environment, rather than merely checking code correctness. While unit and integration tests check the logic and interoperability of Terraform modules, validation tests go a step further: they confirm that, once provisioned, a system meets your functional or business needs. This might include verifying that certain ports are open for traffic, that a web server is responding correctly, or that network latency or replication states match expectations.

Below is an example, using Terratest, that shows how to run a basic validation test against a deployed Azure VM hosting a simple HTTP service.

## Terraform Configuration

Assume you have a **main.tf** that creates a Linux VM in Azure, installs Nginx, and outputs the VM's public IP:

```
provider "azurerm" {
  features {}
}
resource "azurerm_resource_group" "example" {
  name     = "validation-rg"
  location = "EastUS"
}
resource "azurerm_virtual_network" "vnet" {
  name                = "validation-vnet"
```

```
  location            =
azurerm_resource_group.example.location
  resource_group_name = azurerm_resource_group.example.name
  address_space       = ["10.0.0.0/16"]
}
resource "azurerm_subnet" "subnet" {
  name                 = "validation-subnet"
  resource_group_name  = azurerm_resource_group.example.name
  virtual_network_name = azurerm_virtual_network.vnet.name
  address_prefixes     = ["10.0.1.0/24"]
}
resource "azurerm_public_ip" "vm_pip" {
  name                = "validation-pip"
  resource_group_name = azurerm_resource_group.example.name
  location            =
azurerm_resource_group.example.location
  allocation_method   = "Static"
}
resource "azurerm_network_interface" "nic" {
  name                = "validation-nic"
  location            =
azurerm_resource_group.example.location
  resource_group_name = azurerm_resource_group.example.name
  ip_configuration {
    name                          = "testconfiguration"
    subnet_id                     = azurerm_subnet.subnet.id
    private_ip_address_allocation = "Dynamic"
    public_ip_address_id          =
azurerm_public_ip.vm_pip.id
  }
```

```
}
resource "azurerm_linux_virtual_machine" "vm" {
  name                = "validationvm"
  resource_group_name = azurerm_resource_group.example.name
  location            =
azurerm_resource_group.example.location
  size                = "Standard_B1s"
  admin_username      = "azureuser"
  network_interface_ids = [
    azurerm_network_interface.nic.id,
  ]
  disable_password_authentication = false
  admin_password                  = "Password123!"
  # For demonstration: Use provisioners to install Nginx (or
you might rely on cloud-init)
  provisioner "remote-exec" {
    inline = [
      "sudo apt-get update -y",
      "sudo apt-get install -y nginx",
      "sudo systemctl start nginx",
    ]
    connection {
      type        = "ssh"
      user        = "azureuser"
      password    = "Password123!"
      host        = azurerm_public_ip.vm_pip.ip_address
      timeout     = "5m"
    }
  }
}
```

```
output "vm_public_ip" {
  value = azurerm_public_ip.vm_pip.ip_address
}
```

## Validation Test with Terratest

Here, create a file named validation_test.go in a test/ directory:

```
package test
import (
    "fmt"
    "testing"
    "time"
    "github.com/gruntwork-io/terratest/modules/http-helper"
    "github.com/gruntwork-io/terratest/modules/terraform"
    "github.com/stretchr/testify/assert"
)
func TestValidationNginxVM(t *testing.T) {
    t.Parallel()
    // Terraform options referencing the parent directory
    terraformOptions := &terraform.Options{
        TerraformDir: "../",
    }
    // Ensure a cleanup
    defer terraform.Destroy(t, terraformOptions)
    terraform.InitAndApply(t, terraformOptions)
    // Grab the VM's public IP from output
    vmIP := terraform.Output(t, terraformOptions,
"vm_public_ip")
    assert.NotEmpty(t, vmIP, "Public IP output should not be
empty")
```

```
    // Construct the URL to test
    url := fmt.Sprintf("http://%s", vmIP)
    // We expect Nginx to respond with 200 OK
    expectedStatus := 200
    expectedBody := "" // If you want, you can check for some
text
    // For repeated checks
    maxRetries := 10
    timeBetweenRetries := 5 * time.Second
    // Make repeated GET requests to the Nginx service until
success or we exceed maxRetries
    http_helper.HttpGetWithRetry(
        t,
        url,
        expectedStatus,
        expectedBody,
        maxRetries,
        timeBetweenRetries,
    )
}
```

Here in the above code,

- The **terraform.InitAndApply** stands up the entire environment, including the VM that runs Nginx.
- The test retrieves the vm_public_ip from the Terraform output.
- We craft a URL like **http://<public_ip>** and run **HttpGetWithRetry**, verifying we get an HTTP 200 status code. This ensures that Nginx is indeed running.

The test repeats the GET call up to maxRetries times, waiting timeBetweenRetries seconds each time. This accounts for some delay while Nginx finishes installing or the VM finalizes networking.

## Run Test

From the test folder:

```
go test -v
```

If successful, the log indicates each step. If Nginx is misconfigured or the VM took longer to boot, you might see a time-out error or a 404, prompting you to adjust your provisioner or waiting logic.

When you integrate these tests into your pipeline, you systematically ensure that your Terraform-managed environment works in the real world, bridging the gap between "the code looks right" and "the system actually responds as intended".

# Testing Compliance

Compliance testing ensures Terraform configurations meet security, organizational, or regulatory guidelines before changes are deployed. The key is to detect violations—like missing encryption, open TCP ports, or untagged resources—automatically so that undesired changes never reach production. Tools such as Open Policy Agent (OPA), tfsec, or checkov can parse Terraform code or plans and check them against your rules.

Below is an example of using **`Open Policy Agent (OPA)`** to do compliance checks on Terraform's plan.

## Write Rego Policy

Let us say that we want to ensure that all Azure Storage Accounts require TLS 1.2 or above. In older definitions, a user might inadvertently set an insecure property. You create a file policy.rego:

```
package main
deny[msg] {
  input.resource_changes[_].type == "azurerm_storage_account"
  after := input.resource_changes[_].change.after
  after.enable_https_traffic_only == false
  msg := sprintf("Storage account %v must have HTTPS traffic only", [after.name])
}
```

Here, we read each **`resource_changes`** block, look for resources of type azurerm_storage_account, and see if the plan sets **`enable_https_traffic_only`** to false. If so, we issue an error message.

## Generate Terraform Plan in JSON

```
terraform init
terraform plan -out=tfplan
terraform show -json tfplan > tfplan.json
```

Now you have a JSON representation of the plan in **tfplan.json**.

## Evaluate with OPA

Now to evaluate, simply run the following code:

```
opa eval --format pretty \
  --data policy.rego \
  --input tfplan.json \
  "data.main.deny"
```

Here,

- **--data policy.rego** tells OPA to load our Rego policy.
- **--input tfplan.json** tells OPA to evaluate the plan's contents.
- **data.main.deny** tells OPA to print the results of our deny rule.

If no violations occur, the output might be empty or show an empty array. But if someone tried to create or modify a storage account with **enable_https_traffic_only = false**, we might see a message:

```
[
  "Storage account myacct must have HTTPS traffic only"
]
```

## Integrate into CI

To fail the pipeline if any compliance issues are found, check OPA's exit code or parse its output as shown below:

```
RESULT=$(opa eval --format pretty --data policy.rego --input
tfplan.json "data.main.deny")
if [ -n "$RESULT" ]; then
  echo "Compliance check failed: $RESULT"
```

```
  exit 1
fi
```

These final layers of testing complement unit and integration tests, delivering a robust infrastructure testing suite that fosters confidence, reduces risk, and ensures best practices at every step.

# Summary

Overall, this chapter focused on building troubleshooting skills for common Terraform bugs and performance issues. We began by classifying errors into three types - syntax, semantic, and runtime. Practical debugging strategies were presented to address errors head on. We then looked at key Terraform performance metrics, including execution time, resource usage, and code efficiency. We provided use cases to demonstrate performance tuning in action. The ability to import existing resources into Terraform was also covered, allowing pre-provisioned infrastructure to be brought under the management of Terraform. We specifically looked at importing Azure resources to see this capability first hand. The chapter concluded with an in-depth look at testing Terraform code.

# CHAPTER 10: ADMINISTERING TERRAFORM AS EXPERT

# Overview

This chapter is going to go over some of the more complex parts of this powerful tool, focusing on creating modular code components, secrets management, Kubernetes deployment in Azure, and managing container images and metadata. After that, we'll dive into the finer details of actually installing a Kubernetes cluster in Azure, which is the next step. We'll go over the needs, like resource groups, virtual networks, and subnets, as we walk you through the process of building an Azure Kubernetes Service (AKS) cluster. Finally, we'll check out how well Terraform can handle container images and metadata. We'll show how Terraform can create and deploy Kubernetes clusters and apps, as well as manage compute, network, and storage resources, to demonstrate its adaptability.

In general, this chapter shows how Terraform can be used in many different areas of today's technology infrastructure, bringing together Terraform's wide capabilities.

# Create Custom Modules

The creation and sharing of custom modules transforms Terraform from a sprawling collection of .tf files into a clean, maintainable, and reusable code base. They contain logic for provisioning a specific set of related resources. A module in Terraform is essentially a directory of .tf files, variables, and outputs. You can enable different projects and teams to replicate standardized patterns by packaging infrastructure components into modules, which improves consistency and reduces duplicate code. The following is a step-by-step walkthrough for creating and using your own custom modules.

## Identify Reusable Infrastructure Blocks

The first step is to scan your existing Terraform configurations for repeating patterns - for example, a standard virtual machine setup, a database instance with consistent naming and security rules, or a load balancer with identical logic across multiple services. If you find that you're repeatedly copying or modifying the same set of resources for new projects, that's a great fit for a module.

For example, say you have a typical Azure Virtual Machine configuration that needs a network interface, public IP, and security group. Instead of rewriting these resources for each VM, you can package them together in a single module, passing in variables like vm_name or subnet_id.

## Setup Module Directory

First, create a folder to serve as your module. I have used the common pattern as below:

```
modules/
  custom_vm/
```

**main.tf**

**variables.tf**

**outputs.tf**

Inside **`main.tf`**, you then define the core resources:

```
# main.tf
resource "azurerm_network_interface" "nic" {
  name                = var.vm_name
  location            = var.location
  resource_group_name = var.rg_name
  ip_configuration {
    name                          = "ipconfig"
    subnet_id                     = var.subnet_id
    private_ip_address_allocation = "Dynamic"
  }
}
resource "azurerm_public_ip" "pip" {
  name                = "${var.vm_name}-pip"
  location            = var.location
  resource_group_name = var.rg_name
  allocation_method   = "Dynamic"
}
resource "azurerm_linux_virtual_machine" "vm" {
  name                = var.vm_name
  location            = var.location
  resource_group_name = var.rg_name
  size                = var.vm_size
  network_interface_ids = [
    azurerm_network_interface.nic.id
  ]
```

```
  disable_password_authentication = false
  admin_username                  = var.admin_username
  admin_password                  = var.admin_password
}
```

The **`variables.tf`** might define all inputs the module needs:

```
# variables.tf
variable "vm_name" {
  type        = string
  description = "Name for the VM."
}
variable "rg_name" {
  type        = string
  description = "Name of the resource group."
}
variable "location" {
  type        = string
  description = "Azure region."
}
variable "subnet_id" {
  type        = string
  description = "ID of the subnet to attach the VM's NIC."
}
variable "vm_size" {
  type        = string
  default     = "Standard_B1s"
  description = "Size of the virtual machine."
}
variable "admin_username" {
```

```
  type        = string
  default     = "azureuser"
  description = "Admin username for the VM."
}
variable "admin_password" {
  type        = string
  description = "Admin password for the VM."
  sensitive   = true
}
```

And **outputs.tf** could export references:

```
# outputs.tf
output "nic_id" {
  description = "ID of the Network Interface."
  value       = azurerm_network_interface.nic.id
}
output "vm_id" {
  description = "ID of the Azure VM."
  value       = azurerm_linux_virtual_machine.vm.id
}
output "public_ip" {
  description = "Public IP of the VM."
  value       = azurerm_public_ip.pip.ip_address
}
```

## Reference the Module in Main Configuration

In your main Terraform code, you can then reference this module:

```
module "custom_vm" {
  source          = "./modules/custom_vm"
```

```
  vm_name        = "my-special-vm"
  rg_name        = azurerm_resource_group.example.name
  location       = azurerm_resource_group.example.location
  subnet_id      = azurerm_subnet.example.id
  vm_size        = "Standard_DS1_v2"
  admin_username = "devopsuser"
  admin_password = "Secret123!"
}
```

The Terraform then fetches the module from the local path and uses the supplied variable values. Upon **terraform init** and **terraform apply**, the VM, NIC, and PIP get created with minimal repeated code.

## Versioning and Sharing Modules

While you work in a local environment, referencing **source = "./modules/custom_vm"** is enough and quite an essential practice as well. For a distributed team or larger organization, you can store the module in a Git repository or private registry:

```
module "custom_vm" {
  source   = "git::https://github.com/org/terraform-modules.git//azure_vm?ref=v1.2.0"
  vm_name  = "my-special-vm"
  # ...
}
```

Here **ref=v1.2.0** locks a stable version of the module, preventing unexpected changes.

Ultimately, custom modules promote code reuse, accelerate new environment provisioning, and enforce consistent patterns across your team's Terraform deployments.

# HashiCorp Vault and Dynamic Secrets

Managing sensitive credentials in static **.tfvars** or environment variables is risky: passwords might leak, remain unchanged for months, or appear in logs. HashiCorp Vault addresses these threats by issuing short-lived, auto-expiring credentials, known as dynamic secrets. Instead of storing a long-lived password in code, your Terraform configuration can request a credential from

Vault at runtime. Vault then generates ephemeral credentials for the provider—like Azure or a database—and ensures they expire or get revoked after a lease.

Given below is an illustration of how to integrate Terraform with Vault for dynamic secrets:

## Vault to Manage Azure Secrets

Here, first we need to enable and configure the Azure secrets engine in Vault:

```
vault secrets enable azure
vault write azure/config \
    subscription_id="SUBSCRIPTION_ID" \
    tenant_id="TENANT_ID" \
    client_id="CLIENT_ID" \
    client_secret="CLIENT_SECRET"
```

## Create Role with Privileges

Now here, in the Vault, we can define roles that map to specific Azure permissions as shown below:

```
vault write azure/roles/my_contributor_role \
    azure_roles='[
      {
        "role_name": "Contributor",
        "scope": "/subscriptions/12345678-9abc-def0-1234-
56789abcdef0/resourceGroups/example-rg"
      }
    ]'
```

Now, reading **`vault read azure/creds/my_contributor_role`** yields ephemeral credentials with "Contributor" rights in that resource group.

## Integrate Vault into Terraform

You can either retrieve secrets from Vault manually before running Terraform or rely on a custom provider / external data source. For a simple approach, you might store the credentials from Vault in environment variables ephemeral at apply time. Or use a local-exec provisioner that calls Vault's CLI, extracts dynamic credentials, and passes them into variables. For instance:

```
variable "azure_client_id" {}
variable "azure_client_secret" {}
resource "local_file" "temp_creds" {
  content = <<EOT
client_id=${var.azure_client_id}
client_secret=${var.azure_client_secret}
EOT
  filename = "temp_creds.txt"
}
# Hypothetical approach: A local-exec provisioner to read from
Vault, then run Terraform with these credentials
```

The Vault automatically revokes ephemeral credentials after a lease period. Suppose an Azure service principal was created. Once the lease expires, Vault deletes that service principal. This dynamic approach ensures credentials remain valid only as long as needed, drastically limiting an attacker's window if credentials leak.

If your code references ephemeral credentials, you minimize long-term exposure. Even if they leak, they quickly become invalid.

# Managing Kubernetes Resources

You can administer Kubernetes clusters and workloads with Terraform by leveraging the Kubernetes provider. It lets you define your entire application environment – including VMs, networking, and Kubernetes manifests – in one consistent codebase. Instead of applying YAML files with kubectl, you can write Terraform blocks that create or update Kubernetes objects such as namespaces, deployments, services, config maps, etc.

Below is a step-by-step walkthrough to manage Kubernetes resources.

## Declare Kubernetes Provider

In your root module or provider's configuration, set the Kubernetes provider:

```
provider "kubernetes" {
  # If you have a kubeconfig file in the default location,
specifying config_path can suffice
  config_path = "~/.kube/config"
```

```
}
```

You can also pass raw credentials or in-cluster configuration. For instance, if you run Terraform from a pod in the cluster with a service account, you might rely on environment variables or in-cluster config instead of a local config file

## Creating Namespace

A frequent first step is to create a namespace to isolate your workloads:

```
resource "kubernetes_namespace" "example" {
  metadata {
    name = "demo-namespace"
  }
}
```

After **terraform apply**, a new namespace named **demo-namespace** is created in the cluster. If you remove or rename this resource and re-apply, the Terraform will handle updates or deletions accordingly

## Manage Deployments and Services

The Terraform can also create typical Kubernetes resources like Deployments and Services. Here, we will deploy a Nginx container with three replicas, fronted by a ClusterIP service in your new namespace.

```
resource "kubernetes_deployment" "nginx_deployment" {
  metadata {
    name      = "nginx"
    namespace = kubernetes_namespace.example.metadata[0].name
    labels = {
      app = "nginx"
    }
  }
  spec {
    replicas = 3
```

```
    selector {
      match_labels = {
        app = "nginx"
      }
    }
    template {
      metadata {
        labels = {
          app = "nginx"
        }
      }
      spec {
        container {
          name  = "nginx"
          image = "nginx:1.19"
          port {
            container_port = 80
          }
        }
      }
    }
  }
}
resource "kubernetes_service" "nginx_service" {
  metadata {
    name      = "nginx-svc"
    namespace = kubernetes_namespace.example.metadata[0].name
    labels = {
      app = "nginx"
```

```
    }
  }
  spec {
    selector = {
      app = "nginx"
    }
    port {
      port        = 80
      target_port = 80
    }
  }
}
```

Here,

- **kubernetes_deployment** references the same namespace as the previously declared namespace resource, ensuring the pods run in the right place.
- The **`container`** block sets the image for Nginx, with a single container_port of 80.
- The **kubernetes_service** picks up pods with the label app=nginx, routing traffic on port 80.

Finally, we have to run **`terraform apply`** to deploy all these resources. You can also check them with **`kubectl get pods -n demo-namespace`** or **`kubectl get svc -n demo-namespace`**.

## Combining with Other Providers

Now here, a typical situation that may occur is creating the cluster infrastructure with the Azure (or AWS, GCP) provider, then referencing that cluster's credentials or outputs in the Kubernetes provider as below:

```
data "azurerm_kubernetes_cluster" "existing_aks" {
  name                = "MyAKS"
  resource_group_name = "MyResourceGroup"
}
```

```
provider "kubernetes" {
  host                   =
data.azurerm_kubernetes_cluster.existing_aks.kube_config.0.hos
t
  client_certificate     =
base64decode(data.azurerm_kubernetes_cluster.existing_aks.kube
_config.0.client_certificate)
  client_key             =
base64decode(data.azurerm_kubernetes_cluster.existing_aks.kube
_config.0.client_key)
  cluster_ca_certificate =
base64decode(data.azurerm_kubernetes_cluster.existing_aks.kube
_config.0.cluster_ca_certificate)
}
```

The above program queries an existing AKS cluster for its connection data, then sets up the **kubernetes** provider accordingly. Next, you can create your Nginx deployment in that same module to have consistent management from the cluster's underlying resources up to the actual workloads.

# Reference Image Metadata

When it comes to provisioning virtual machines in the cloud, specifying the base image is really important. In Azure, for example, you could choose a marketplace image like Ubuntu 20.04 or Windows Server 2019. Or, you might have a custom "managed image" or a shared image from your own gallery. Inside Terraform, referencing image metadata ensures that your VMs start with the correct operating system or baseline configuration.

Given below are two main ways to handle images in Azure:

## Using Marketplace Image

The Azure's marketplace images require a publisher, offer, sku, and version as shown below:

```
resource "azurerm_linux_virtual_machine" "vm_marketplace" {
  name                = "marketplace-ubuntu-vm"
  resource_group_name = azurerm_resource_group.example.name
```

```
  location            =
azurerm_resource_group.example.location
  size                = "Standard_B1s"
  admin_username      = "azureuser"
  # The image reference from Azure Marketplace
  source_image_reference {
    publisher = "Canonical"
    offer     = "UbuntuServer"
    sku       = "18.04-LTS"
    version   = "latest"
  }
  network_interface_ids = [
    azurerm_network_interface.example.id
  ]
  admin_password = "MyP@ssw0rd"
}
```

The Terraform directly references the known marketplace metadata for Ubuntu 18.04. The **`version = "latest"`** ensures it always picks the newest patch-level image from that SKU. If you want to pin a specific version, replace **`latest`** with an explicit version number.

## Referencing a Managed Image

Perhaps you have your own custom image stored as a "managed image" in Azure. Now say you have created an image that contains pre-installed software for your application. In that case, you'd need to define a data block to read the existing image.

```
data "azurerm_image" "my_custom_image" {
  name                = "myCustomImage"
  resource_group_name = "myImageResourceGroup"
}
resource "azurerm_linux_virtual_machine" "vm_custom" {
  name                = "custom-image-vm"
```

```
  resource_group_name = azurerm_resource_group.example.name
  location            =
azurerm_resource_group.example.location
  size                = "Standard_B2s"
  admin_username      = "azureuser"
  admin_password      = "AnotherP@ssW0rd"
  network_interface_ids = [
    azurerm_network_interface.example.id
  ]
  # source_image_id references the ID from the data block
  source_image_id = data.azurerm_image.my_custom_image.id
}
```

Here, the **data "azurerm_image" "my_custom_image"** retrieves metadata for the custom image from the specified resource group. And, the VM references that image's ID in its **source_image_id** property, launching new VMs from it. So even if you update or rename the custom image, you only tweak the data block while the rest remains stable.

## For AWS and GCP

Now on AWS, referencing an AMI is commonly done with a data block like:

```
data "aws_ami" "ubuntu" {
  most_recent = true
  owners      = ["099720109477"] # Canonical
  filter {
    name   = "name"
    values = ["ubuntu/images/hvm-ssd/ubuntu-focal-20.04-amd64-
server-*"]
  }
}
resource "aws_instance" "ubuntu_vm" {
  ami             = data.aws_ami.ubuntu.id
```

```
  instance_type = "t2.micro"
  # ...
}
```

Similarly, GCP has a data block for images. The concept is the same: rely on a data source to fetch the correct image metadata and then feed it into your compute resource.

# Provision AKS Cluster

The deployment of an AKS cluster via Terraform unifies the cluster setup with the rest of your IaC approach. Instead of creating a resource group, subnets, and the AKS cluster in the Azure portal (or mixing them with separate CLI commands), it does it all in a single, repeatable flow.

The following is a step-by-step walkthrough, showing both the required Azure resources and the final creation of the AKS cluster.

## Define Resource Group and Networking

AKS requires a resource group for the cluster itself. You will typically create one resource group that houses the cluster and its associated resources. Likewise, you must define virtual network settings if you want to assign pods or nodes to your own subnets.

```
provider "azurerm" {
  features {}
}
resource "azurerm_resource_group" "aks_rg" {
  name     = "aks-resource-group"
  location = "West Europe"
}
resource "azurerm_virtual_network" "aks_vnet" {
  name                = "aks-vnet"
  location            = azurerm_resource_group.aks_rg.location
  resource_group_name = azurerm_resource_group.aks_rg.name
  address_space       = ["10.100.0.0/16"]
}
```

```
resource "azurerm_subnet" "aks_subnet" {
  name                 = "aks-subnet"
  resource_group_name  = azurerm_resource_group.aks_rg.name
  virtual_network_name = azurerm_virtual_network.aks_vnet.name
  address_prefixes     = ["10.100.1.0/24"]
}
```

## Create AKS Cluster

With the resource group and networking in place, define **azurerm_kubernetes_cluster**:

```
resource "azurerm_kubernetes_cluster" "aks_cluster" {
  name                = "my-aks-cluster"
  location            = azurerm_resource_group.aks_rg.location
  resource_group_name = azurerm_resource_group.aks_rg.name
  dns_prefix          = "my-aks"
  default_node_pool {
    name       = "nodepool1"
    node_count = 3
    vm_size    = "Standard_DS2_v2"
    vnet_subnet_id = azurerm_subnet.aks_subnet.id
  }
  identity {
    type = "SystemAssigned"
  }
  # This example uses the 'RBAC with AKS-managed Azure AD'
approach
  role_based_access_control {
    enabled = true
  }
  # Enable network plugin, typically 'azure' or 'kubenet'
```

```
  network_profile {
    network_plugin     = "azure"
    load_balancer_sku = "standard"
    dns_service_ip     = "10.100.2.10"
    service_cidr       = "10.100.2.0/24"
    docker_bridge_cidr = "172.17.0.1/16"
  }
}
```

Now in the above script,

- **dns_prefix** is used for your AKS control plane endpoint.
- **default_node_pool** defines a single node pool named nodepool1 with three nodes, each a **Standard_DS2_v2** VM. The **vnet_subnet_id** references your previously created subnet.
- **role_based_access_control.enabled** allows more secure cluster access using Azure AD or Kubernetes RBAC.
- And, finally the **network_profile** dictates how pods get network addresses, how load balancing works, etc. With network_plugin = "azure," each pod can get an IP in the vnet. The snippet also sets internal addresses for cluster services.

After writing this, run **`terraform init`** and **`terraform apply`**. The cluster creation process typically takes several minutes, as Azure must spin up the control plane and node VMs.

## Obtain Cluster Credentials

Post-deployment, you likely want to administer the cluster with **`kubectl`** or CI/CD systems using Azure CLI as below:

```
az aks get-credentials --resource-group aks-resource-group --
name my-aks-cluster
kubectl get nodes
```

This merges the cluster's kubeconfig into your default **`~/.kube/config`** file so **`kubectl`** can connect.

Now we also know that by default, **`azurerm_kubernetes_cluster`** can output certain fields, or you can define your own outputs to fetch the cluster certificate, endpoint, or token. However, you must parse them manually or feed them into a **`kubernetes`** provider if you want

Terraform to manage deployments on the cluster as shown below.

```
output "kube_config" {
  value =
azurerm_kubernetes_cluster.aks_cluster.kube_config_raw
  sensitive = true
}
```

Then after **`terraform apply`**, you can run **`terraform output kube_config`** to retrieve the config (base64-encoded or raw, depending on your resource blocks). Decoding it and saving it to a file can let you use that as a KUBECONFIG.

With all the above steps, you unify cluster creation, node configuration, networking, plus the eventual workloads for consistent, code-driven infrastructure. This drastically simplifies large-scale or multi-team Azure deployments, fosters more reliable upgrades, and ensures your cluster is recreated predictably if you must rebuild or replicate it in a new region.

# Summary

To sum up our learning in this last chapter, we looked into different ways to create reusable, modular pieces of code, also known as Terraform modules. We saw how HashiCorp Vault can safely manage sensitive information and secrets. Instead of using static keys and passwords, teams can use Vault's ability to generate temporary credentials in a dynamic way.

Then, we set up a Kubernetes cluster on Microsoft Azure's cloud platform and walked through creating an AKS cluster by specifying the necessary components like resource groups, virtual networks, and subnets. We then explored how Terraform can be used to manage container images and metadata. Finally, we saw firsthand how Terraform empowers infrastructure teams by providing a standardized and unified workflow across the entire stack, from low-level cloud resources to container-based services.

# Index

## A



## C



## D



## E



## G



## H



## I



## K



## L



## N



## O



## P



## R

## S



## T



## U



## V

# Epilogue

Hopefully, by now, you can see the transformation that happens when managing infrastructure with Terraform. With this second edition, I have shown you not only how to write code to create virtual machines and subnets, but also how to weave in dynamic secrets, ephemeral environments, and even container orchestration. The point was to show that provisioning is not just about telling the cloud, "Create this server. It's about orchestrating every piece, from credentials that expire automatically to pipelines that run tests before changes go live.

Each chapter demonstrated real-world scenarios where automation and consistent provisioning reduce errors. We also looked at some advanced stuff, like modules that combine code patterns, so you don't have to repeat the same blocks every time you set up a new environment. This kind of approach makes your infrastructure maintainable at scale, and gives you confidence that every change is versioned and thoroughly tested before deployment. We also learned that credentials from systems like Vault that are only valid for a short time help keep our operations secure, and test environments that are only used for a short time ensure that we can test changes on copies of production environments before affecting actual users.

But the most important thing to know is that this edition focuses on real tasks, like bridging subnets, setting up container images, and integrating Kubernetes clusters, which can all be done with Terraform. With these lessons, you reduce the manual overhead that once burdened network engineering, operations teams, and compliance reviews. It gets rid of all that guesswork and makes sure each step is documented and reproducible.

I encourage you to keep experimenting with the patterns we uncovered. Tweak them for your own cloud environments, build more robust pipelines, and keep refining how secrets are handled.

***The more you use Terraform's automation, the less your team will have to deal with random changes, and the more your infrastructure will become a solid base for new ideas.***

***---Kimiko Lee***

# Thank You

www.ingramcontent.com/pod-product-compliance
Lightning Source LLC
Chambersburg PA
CBHW080215170726
48282CB00030B/1123
* 9 7 8 8 1 1 9 1 7 7 8 6 8 *